Words of Life

The Bible Day by Day
September–December 2012

HODDER &
STOUGHTON

First published in Great Britain in 2012 by Hodder & Stoughton
An Hachette UK company

Copyright © 2012 by The Salvation Army
International Headquarters, 101 Queen Victoria Street,
London EC4V 4EH

1

A CIP catalogue record for this title is available from the British Library

ISBN 978 1 444 70264 4
eBook ISBN 978 1 444 70349 8

Typeset in Sabon and Scala Sans by Avon DataSet Ltd,
Bidford on Avon, Warwickshire

Printed and bound in Great Britain
by Clays Ltd, St Ives plc

Hodder & Stoughton policy is to use papers that are natural, renewable
and recyclable products and made from wood grown in sustainable forests.
The logging and manufacturing processes are expected to conform to the
environmental regulations of the country of origin.

Hodder & Stoughton Ltd
338 Euston Road
London NW1 3BH

www.hodderfaith.com

Contents

From the writer of *Words of Life*

Living our Faith

It's a beautiful thing to meditate upon God's Word with fellow-believers! Welcome to this time of communion with our Lord and Saviour, Jesus Christ. This year we have been exploring the concept of faith. This edition looks to 'Living our Faith', as we walk with Christ daily.

We begin with the powerful book of Isaiah – and all it has to say to us regarding our faith walk in today's world. We move on to the prophetic book of Daniel, a man of great faith. Then, four minor prophets: Amos, Micah, Zephaniah and Haggai, all living out their faith during difficult times of judgment.

In the New Testament we look at letters to the Galatians, Colossians and Titus – followed by letters from James and Jude. Also, there are two short series on the fruit of the Spirit as well as various aspects of faith. Our guest writer for this edition – Captain Julius Omukonyi from Kenya – leads us into the Christmas season.

Again, a look at various psalms, proverbs and hymns of the Church causes us to reflect upon how we live out our faith in daily interaction with others. Martin Luther King Jr told us to 'take the first step in faith. You don't have to see the whole staircase; just take the first step.'

I pray God will richly bless you as you prepare for celebrating, once again, the birth of Jesus. And as we share in *living our faith* together in these daily readings, let's allow Christ to reveal himself to us in a new and intimate way.

May the Lord Christ – *Immanuel* – continue to be 'with you' as you meditate daily upon his Word.

Beverly Ivany
Toronto, Canada

Abbreviations

My Shepherd

The LORD is my shepherd, I shall not be in want (v. 1).

We commence this edition of *Words of Life* with the psalm that is perhaps the most treasured in all of the Psalter. Why do we resonate so clearly with it? Because we're all sheep, in desperate need of a shepherd.

Sheep, not the brightest of animals, have a way of constantly getting lost. When grazing in a pasture, they often begin to wander. After all, the grass is always greener on the other side of the fence! It's the shepherd who makes the difference. The Lord is *my* Shepherd – a personal declaration of a valued relationship.

I've never been exposed much to sheep. But recently I visited the beautiful country of Wales. There, sheep are spotted on the hillsides – everywhere! At one point I even saw a lone black sheep, in the midst of all the white ones. I immediately thought of 'the black sheep of the family' concept. But the sheep I saw was not ostracised in any way. It was included – all sheep grazing together. No matter the colour of our skin, our background, our social status, our Shepherd loves us equally. We're all his treasured sheep!

He wants us, his sheep, to lie down in *green pastures*, where the *quiet waters* bring comfort. Despite any storms that might come, the Shepherd commits to bringing and imparting peace and stillness. He then wants to *restore* our soul. In today's frantic world we need restoration; we need to be led in the way of *righteousness*. As we trust God, completely, we see the *path* he has for us.

The trust that is built in the relationship, Shepherd with sheep, prepares us for the *valley of the shadow of death*. We have the constant assurance that he's with us and will never forsake us – even through the very difficult times of life. For his *rod and staff* keep us in balance. When enemies come, we have the strength to turn them away. And when we do, we celebrate by feasting at the prepared *table*.

Finally, the Shepherd *anoints* us, and our cup *overflows* with his blessings. Because of this, *goodness and love* follow us – and will throughout eternity. Yes, this is our Shepherd – *my* beautiful Shepherd!

Battle Hymn

*Some trust in chariots and some in horses, but we trust in the name of the
LORD our God (v. 7).*

The patriotic hymn, 'Battle Hymn of the Republic', was penned by
American writer Julia Ward Howe in 1861. She used the tune associated
with the song 'John Brown's Body' – so titled because the abolitionist, Brown,
was hanged, wanting freedom for slaves.

> Mine eyes have seen the glory of the coming of the Lord;
> He is trampling out the vintage where the grapes of wrath are stored;
> He hath loosed the fateful lightning of his terrible swift sword;
> His truth is marching on.
>
> *(SASB 162)*

The above words came to Julia, for she wanted freedom and liberty for *all*
people. The battle rages on, even today, against injustices in our world.
Christians worldwide need to speak up, declaring God's truth to all nations;
to speak of his righteousness and goodness.

It's a battle out there. But many don't see it. People can become
complacent when it comes to faith. We can even, at times, give up in our
desire to bring others to Christ. But the Lord at no time gives up. He sounds
the trumpet, wanting us never to retreat from the battle that's to be won. It's
a matter of life and death.

> He has sounded forth the trumpet that shall never call retreat;
> He is sifting out the hearts of men before his judgment seat;
> O be swift, my soul, to answer him, be jubilant my feet!
> Our God is marching on.
>
> *(v. 3)*

> Glory, glory, hallelujah! His truth is marching on.
> *(refrain)*

Let's live each day with the desire to set people free in Christ!

Isaiah the Man

'Though your sins are like scarlet, they shall be as white as snow' (v. 18).

Today we begin to look at Isaiah, a book of Hebrew prophecy. The first thirty-nine chapters (relating to the thirty-nine books of the Old Testament) stress the righteousness and holiness of God – announcing his judgment and condemnation upon a world stained *scarlet* with sin. The last twenty-seven chapters (relating to the twenty-seven books of the New Testament) portray God's compassion and consolation for his people. Messiah *will* come as Saviour, bearing a cross; and as Sovereign, wearing a crown.

At the end of the eighth century BC, Isaiah comes on the scene as God's human instrument, speaking to and challenging the nation. Being well educated and from a prominent Jewish family, Isaiah was used by God to be a prophet – for such a time as this.

Wickedness was all around him, having deeply permeated into every fibre of the social, political and spiritual life of the country. God finds this intolerable. Unless there is repentance, God will reduce his people to ruin. Isaiah's funeral dirge over Jerusalem (as you read on from v. 20) speaks to the nation's spiritual revolt:

See how the faithful city has become a harlot! She once was full of justice; righteousness used to dwell in her (v. 21).

Does it sound familiar? Many cities today, once beautiful and inviting, are now full of corruption; polluted with sin, greed, crime. Many of us often feel at a loss. What can we do to bring about change? Isaiah was an insider, one of the people. As he was compelled to relay a message of warning to his people, God gave a glimmer of hope: *'There's a day coming . . .'* (2:2, MSG). For Isaiah, it was a magnificent, spectacular dream. To one day have peace; to be walking *in the light of the LORD* (2:5, NIV).

Let's dream big – trusting everything to God; then being ready, like Isaiah, to be used for God's glory.

The Branch

In that day the Branch of the LORD will be beautiful and glorious, and the fruit of the land will be the pride and glory of the survivors in Israel (v. 2).

There's punishment for sin. But, with repentance, there's also hope. For the Israelites, it wasn't just an escape from judgment; not just withholding condemnation for sin and wickedness. There was the real hope of the Messiah: the *Branch* would one day come, bringing salvation for all humankind.

The Messiah springs from a dual ancestry – that of David and God himself. The human side of his ancestry is significant; but even more important is his divine ancestry, arising out of the heavenly realm.

Following the oracles of doom, coming from the people's sins, we have this promise of restoration. It's a blessing, giving them great hope for the days that lie ahead.

The people will be won back by experiencing God's power, forgiveness, and grace.

It's all possible, no matter what we've done in life, because of this *Branch*. Messiah brings hope, forgiveness, salvation, eternity:

'Here is the man whose name is the Branch . . . he will be clothed with majesty and will sit and rule on his throne' (Zechariah 6:12, 13).

The *Branch* was not just for the people during the time of Isaiah. He is for us, bringing righteousness and holiness, desiring us to be part of him – now, and forever.

'I will raise up to David a righteous Branch . . . This is the name by which he will be called: The LORD Our Righteousness' (Jeremiah 23:5, 6).

The prophecy of this promised *Branch* brought such hope to the people. This same *Branch* has come – bringing salvation to the world. And he's coming again, to bring us home to be with him. Let's make sure we're ready for his coming.

Call and Commission

'Holy, holy, holy is the LORD *Almighty; the whole earth is full of his glory'*
(v. 3).

A lthough Isaiah might have commenced his ministry a few years earlier, he was called to a *unique* ministry in the year of King Uzziah's death, 740 BC. He received a vision from God, which determined the course of his life. Yet he felt so unworthy, even feeling his lips were unable to adequately speak of God's holiness. But God wanted him to be a prophet, his instrument.

Isaiah knew that, through God's power, a transformation *could* take place within him. He also believed a transformation could take place within the people themselves. If they turned from their rebellious ways, desiring God's holiness, they would be changed. But this all had to begin within the one delivering the message – Isaiah. He needed to respond to God's call upon his own life, believing – through God's Spirit – he could and *would* be used for his service.

Responding to God's call begins by kneeling before the King of kings, realising the awesomeness of God; coming to grips with one's own sinfulness before confronting others with the same, *'Woe to me! . . . I am a man of unclean lips'* (v. 5).

The seraph came to Isaiah, bringing a live coal from the altar. He touched the prophet's lips, cleansing him completely. A powerful image! Not just for Isaiah, but for you, for me. The live coal, touching *our* lips – so that all we do and say brings glory to God.

It is then that the commission comes: to tell the people of God's saving grace. We are to respond:

'Here am I. Send me!' (v. 8).

Oh, the majesty and holiness of our God! Let's look up, in praise to him, and envision the Lord on his throne. Can you see him? Let us say, together: '*Holy, holy, holy is the* LORD *Almighty.*'

Freedom through God's Grace

Brothers and sisters, I want you to know that the gospel I preached isn't human in origin . . . It came through a revelation from Jesus Christ (vv. 11, 12, CEB).

Celtic or Gaelic masses moved eastward from Western Europe during the 400 years between the Old and New Testaments. One such group moved into Asia Minor, carving out a state called Galatia. Paul established new churches in that region; but time had since passed – enough for certain things to develop which needed to be addressed. Reactionary Jewish teachers had been unwilling to accept the decision of the Jerusalem Council that all were welcome into full relationship with Christ. They were being legalistic. Paul writes, trying to save the Galatians from apostasy. He begins by defending his own apostleship:

From Paul, an apostle who is not sent from human authority . . . but sent through Jesus Christ and God the Father (v. 1, CEB).

He then wants to stress the supremacy of the gospel: the importance of both the law and the new promise given by Christ. Paul wants the Galatians to be *free*, living their lives in God's grace.

Freedom is a beautiful word – and especially as it relates to faith. All of us can so easily get caught up in legalism in the Church, losing sight of the true gospel and the liberty it brings for all people. We're to accept God's blessings for each of us.

This letter to the Galatians declares a gospel of freedom through God's grace. It was a revelation to be embraced by both Jews and Gentiles. God called Paul, as he called the Galatians. He calls each of us, personally, by *his grace* (v. 15). Oh yes, we are indeed free in him!

Prayer

Thank you, Lord, for my total freedom in you today!

Living by Faith

*They saw that I had been entrusted with the task of preaching the gospel
to the Gentiles, just as Peter had been to the Jews (v. 7).*

Paul used strategy as well as prayer. He knew that reaching out to Gentiles, and fully embracing them into faith, was new and radical. But it was of God. And so, he went to the leaders who were somewhat in opposition, trying to coerce them privately that preaching to the Gentiles was valid and right.

Titus was a perfect example of one accepted into the fellowship, by God's grace, as a Gentile. The other apostles acknowledged this, so Paul shares this with the sceptical Galatians. It came down to the fundamental question: Were the Gentiles saved by faith in Christ or were they not? The gospel states that we are not justified by the works of the law but through faith in Jesus Christ. Therefore we are to be Christians living by faith, day to day, as we walk with Christ:

*I have been crucified with Christ and I no longer live, but Christ lives in me.
The life I live in the body, I live by faith in the Son of God, who loved me and
gave himself for me (v. 20).*

Living by faith is about trust in God – for the big things, for the small things. It's about having the assurance that God will meet our every need. Then, it's about sharing this profound truth with others – from all walks of life. We're all in this together; for he lives within each one of us.

Living by faith embraces the truth that God loves us, and gave of himself for us. How personal! How intimate! And if he loves us that much, how can we do anything less than live by faith in him? To trust him; to realise he is with us – and will be – day by day.

Prayer

Father, I realise what you've done for me. Help me, in response, to love you more and more; to be a person who is seen to be living by faith. I no longer live, because Christ lives in me. Hallelujah!

King of Glory

The earth is the LORD's, and all it contains, The world, and those who dwell in it (v. 1, NASB).

Psalms 22, 23 and 24 form a trilogy. In Psalm 22, the psalmist first looks to the Saviour's *cross*. Psalm 23 speaks to the Shepherd's *call*. Psalm 24 looks to the Saviour's *celebration* – for one day we'll be with him in glory. In other words, the past, present and the future.

The Lord reigns over *all*; the earth, the universe, everything humans can identify that exists, and even beyond. We're all included here, for we're part of God's world. People may try to conquer lands, fight for territories, and battle for their rights in militaristic ways. But everything belongs to the Lord. When will humankind realise this?

If we believe it *is* God's world, what are we doing to protect it? Do we care enough for the environment? Do we strive to make the world even more beautiful – caring for the vegetation and animal life, making sure the water is clean, sharing our food with others?

We have a moral obligation to be caretakers, stewards of God's world. And as we care for creation, so much more should we be caring for one another. We must do so with *clean hands and a pure heart* (24:4) – to have a holy desire. If we do this:

They will receive blessing from the LORD and vindication from God their Savior (v. 5, TNIV).

We are to be a generation that longs to follow God's direction and lead. One mission. One message. Are we up for this? Do we want to be part of a holy revival? Excitement is in the air; the Spirit *is* moving! Do we sense the presence of the King of Glory today?

Who is this King of glory? The LORD of hosts, He is the King of glory. Selah (v. 10, NASB).

Praise, my Soul

I will praise you, O LORD, among the nations; I will sing of you among the peoples (v. 3).

This anthem, written by Henry Francis Lyte of the nineteenth century, was based on Psalm 108 – a hymn of praise to the King of Heaven:

Praise, my soul, the King of Heaven, To his feet thy tribute bring;
Ransomed, healed, restored, forgiven, Who like thee his praise should sing?
Praise him! Praise the everlasting King.

(SASB 17)

Child psychologists tell us we need to praise our children more for what they do – to build their self-esteem. Marriage counsellors encourage us to praise our spouse, for who they are – to enhance their self-worth. But do we daily give praise to God for the grace he gives to us? Praise for his faithfulness toward us, day after day?

Praise him for his grace and favour To our fathers in distress;
Praise him still the same as ever, Slow to chide and swift to bless;
Praise him! Glorious in his faithfulness.

(v. 2)

Things confront us; people hurt us. When God comes to our rescue, holding us, showing mercy toward us, do we thank and praise him for his Father-like love toward us? He's a wonderful God! The angels know it. Creation knows it. We also know it. And one day, if we prove to be faithful, we'll see him face-to-face. Until then, let's never forget to continuously give praise to our Lord and Saviour!

Angels in the heights adore him, Ye behold him face to face;
Sun and moon bow down before him: Dwellers all in time and space,
Praise him! Praise with us the God of grace.

(v. 4)

Immanuel

'Therefore the Lord himself will give you a sign: The virgin will be with child and will give birth to a son, and will call him Immanuel' (v. 14).

The task set before Isaiah is a great one; for the Lord tells him the people are spiritually deaf and near-sighted. Armed with confidence in his God, Isaiah begins declaring harsh words from on high – even to the courts and palaces in Judah. It was a message of judgment; but it was also a plea for holiness. If the people stopped their rebellion, repenting of their sinful ways, then there was great hope for them – in the midst of all the heartache.

Judah was facing a national crisis. King Ahaz, the grandson of King Uzziah, feared that the Syro-Ephramite coalition would soon overthrow their nation. Ahaz was shaken by this impending threat, as were the people. Isaiah's message was to be *careful* and to stay *calm*. These two threatening nations were like smouldering stubs of firewood. They would not last or survive. Judah, however, *would* survive – but only if it adhered to God's command:

'If you do not stand firm in your faith, you will not stand at all' (v. 9).

But King Ahaz wanted to take things into his own hands. When Isaiah pleaded with him to ask God for a sign, his pride made him refuse. It would take too much humility. Even the pagan gods became more real, to the point of Ahaz sacrificing his son to them:

He . . . sacrificed his son in the fire, following the detestable ways of the nations the Lord *had driven out before the Israelites (2 Kings 16:3).*

Ahaz refused to trust God, choosing to execute his own plan. He desired no sign; but God gave him one anyway. He told the people of the coming of *Immanuel* – meaning 'God with us'. The sign was for then; but it's also an affirmation for us today. God is *with* us, always.

Prince of Peace

For to us a child is born, to us a son is given, and the government will be on his shoulders (v. 6).

When we read today's Scripture verse, many of us will immediately think of the great Baroque composer, Handel, and his momentous oratorio, *Messiah*. The majestic music he set for this powerful passage truly lifts the soul heavenward:

Wonderful Counsellor, Mighty God, Everlasting Father, Prince of Peace (v. 6).

The redeemed can sing his praises, for the ultimate victory is sure.

The Hebrew word translated *Wonderful* is never used of humans or their works, but only of God. Later on in Isaiah, it describes the Lord himself as *wonderful in counsel* (28:29). Messiah is above all, the one who gives to us wisdom and direction in life.

Messiah is also *Mighty God*, for he is part of the Trinity – strong, wise, all-knowing, all-powerful, victorious; but this *Mighty God* also cares about the little things of life.

His love is *everlasting*. Our *Everlasting Father* never fails to provide help in times of trouble; he never fails to supply all our needs; he never neglects his responsibilities.

He is the *Prince of Peace*. Not just bringing an end to war, but one who brings true spiritual peace into the hearts of men and women – no matter what transpires around us. This same *Prince of Peace* will come and sit upon the throne of David for all of eternity:

He will reign on David's throne and over his kingdom, establishing and upholding it with justice and righteousness (v. 7).

God himself will accomplish this. Nothing in the world can hinder it. How great, how great is our God!

The Peaceable Kingdom

A shoot will come up from the stump of Jesse; from his roots a Branch will bear fruit (v. 1).

Although King Ahaz fears what lies ahead, Isaiah warns him of the outcome. Judah, in fact, will appear as a *stump*. As dead. Yet, by the power of God, a *shoot* will spring forth; and from its roots, a *Branch* – bearing fruit. One day, says Isaiah, this Branch will bring resolution and completion, a transformation like nothing else. It will bring renewed hope and promise; new life.

In this beautiful messianic passage, Isaiah lists what the *Spirit* of the Lord will bring to each person who believes in him:

Wisdom and understanding . . . counsel and of power . . . knowledge and of the fear of the LORD (v. 2).

Believers will have the practical ability to reach others, and will be given spiritual insight – for we'll be filled with the holiness of God. We will have spiritual gifts, enabling us to relate to a world in need of Christ.

Isaiah speaks of a peaceable kingdom to come, where there is absolute peace, harmony, tranquillity, love. The world at present is in chaos. Leaders of nations crave for more and more power – at the expense of anything and anyone standing in the way. The Prince of Peace brings *perfect* peace by undoing the effects of sin.

One day, we will see peace among the animals. Little children will be leading them! It's an idyllic picture, for this is what creation was like in the beginning. One day there'll be peace among the nations; reconciliation among all people, all creation:

The wolf will live with the lamb, the leopard will lie down with the goat, the calf and the lion and the yearling together; and a little child will lead them (v. 6).

No more racism, prejudice, abuse, violence. No more hatred, wickedness, evil. No more jealousy, envy, poverty, injustice. No more social disorder. A peaceable kingdom. Lord, let it begin with me!

Foolishness

You foolish Galatians! Who has bewitched you? (v. 1).

Have you ever been foolish? Done foolish things? Have you ever done things that are not godly? We don't often use the word *bewitched*, for it's a strong word. Yet when we turn our eyes away from Christ, we *do* become bewitched – completely off focus. We can become so foolish that we blatantly sin, grieving God's heart.

Some people believe in a basic *moralism*, thinking that following the Golden Rule is enough. A simple guideline for living from day to day, without hurting others. Nothing deep or complicated – asking for little commitment. Just follow a few rules.

Some think *humanism* is the answer. Reason things out. Look out for others here and there, for that's what life's all about.

Others take the *social* or *environmental* approach to life. Improve the climate, the atmosphere. Provide nicer homes. Clean up the cities. Save energy. Build shelters for the homeless.

All of the above are good objectives. But the sole purpose and meaning for life? That's plain foolishness. The gospel, Paul says, is so much more. It's about the centrality of life: the cross, Christ's love, eternal life.

- *Convictions* They're essential – to know not only what's right and wrong, but to live a holy life, pleasing to God alone.
- *Confidence* It's vital for our spiritual life – to keep strong in our faith, having confidence in Christ alone.
- *Cross* This is about our redemption – available for all, which includes both Jew and Gentile.

He redeemed us in order that the blessing given to Abraham might come to the Gentiles through Christ Jesus, so that by faith we might receive the promise of the Spirit (v. 14).

We might do foolish things. But let's never be foolish when it comes to our relationship with our Lord.

Abandonment

What has happened to all your joy? (v. 15).

There's nothing quite like seeing someone come to Christ and showing evidence of joy, freedom, release, forgiveness, change, transformation. They glow – because the Spirit of God now dwells within them. They're adopted into the family of God, becoming new in Christ. Nothing can compare! Then time passes. The joy gradually dissipates. The exuberance, lost. The Christian walk becomes mundane. What's happened?

Paul shows his genuine concern as he questions the Galatians in his letter, saying to them: How can you slip back into your old ways, the way you were living before you knew Christ? Maybe not committing blatant sins; but being, as Paul says, in a state of slavery to the old life, the old way of living. He then says to them: *I fear for you* (v. 11).

He makes a personal appeal, for he genuinely cares for his *brothers* (v. 12). He longs for them to be revitalised in their spirit. To not be bound, but to be free. To experience complete abandonment.

I love my husband, Dave. He's much more daring than I am. But he gently pushes me to move beyond any fears I might have. And so, one day, we went white-water rafting. It was one of the best experiences I've ever had. And I lived to tell the tale! Rapids. Gushing water. Speed. Fear. Fabulous! Yes, Dave was concerned for my safety, and could understand my hesitation at first. But because he cares for me, I trusted him. It was an exhilarating experience – complete abandonment.

Having the joy of the Lord within is far more than this. It's something to be *greatly* treasured. And it is so revitalising and invigorating! Perhaps reliving a conversion experience might be necessary, to make sure Christ's joy overflows in our own life.

May we be sensitive to God's leading. May we be people of encouragement to others as we come alongside and walk with our brothers and sisters. It's about showing concern, compassion, care. It's about complete abandonment – in Christ!

A Portrait of Christ

'I love those who love me, and those who seek me find me' (v. 17).

There's something quite striking and very personal about this proverb. Many scholars see this passage as prophetical, looking ahead to Christ's incarnation. Theologian Charles Fritsch says this Scripture is 'one of the most perfect pictures of Christ to be found in the Old Testament . . . a portraiture of the essential wisdom of God personified'.[1] Christ, personified as wisdom, says:

'I walk in the way of righteousness, along the paths of justice' (v. 20).

When God asked King Solomon what he wanted, the king could have asked for wealth or fame. Instead he asked for wisdom. He wanted to be a good ruler; to be godly in his way of dealing with people. He wanted to make wise decisions, according to God's will (see 1 Kings 3:5–9).

This proverb indicates that desiring godly wisdom is wanting to be Christlike in character; for seeking wisdom from God is virtually to reflect a portrait of who Christ is – who he always was:

'I was there when he set the heavens in place, when he marked out the horizon on the face of the deep . . . and when he marked out the foundations of the earth' (Proverbs 8:27, 29).

We need to daily ask for God's wisdom; for we need to be more like Christ. When our heart and mind is in tune with our Lord, then choices we make will be wise choices. Today, let's look to the portrait of Christ – asking him what he would have us do to honour him:

'For whoever finds me finds life' (v. 35).

Prayer

Dear Father, thank you for your Son. Thank you for the gift of wisdom. Help me to be wise and to always reflect your glory.

Is It Nothing?

'Is it nothing to you, all you who pass by?' (v. 12).

> Is it nothing to you that one day Jesus came
> All our sorrow and suffering to share?
> He came as the light of new hope for a world
> In the day of its darkest despair.
>
> *(SASB 245)*

This hymn was born out of the haunting question: 'Is it nothing to you?' In the mid-twentieth century, Albert Mingay was sitting on a train looking at people bustling from one place to another in a very busy city. What meaning did the gospel have for them? What thought did they have of the crucified Christ – the giver of new life?

We can all become so caught up in busy lifestyles that we, too, can fail to stop and simply focus all our thoughts on our Lord:

> Is it nothing to you that today Jesus saves?
> Though we stand all condemned before God
> He carries our sin on his own loving heart,
> And he saves by his pardoning blood.
>
> *(v. 4)*

Jesus gave his life. For you, for me; for the people in our cities and communities. Although condemned because of our sin, we're pardoned, forgiven. When we call out to him, he's there for us. He wants to walk with us, when we are going through difficulties. He wants to comfort us, when sickness or tragedy strikes. He wants to carry us, when we don't have the strength to move forward. He wants to forgive us, taking our guilt away. Jesus is everything!

> Is it nothing to you that his cross speaks our shame?
> Is it nothing to you, for whose cleansing he came,
> That our guilt made his Calvary and pierced his hands through?
> Is it nothing to you? Is it nothing, nothing to you?
>
> *(refrain)*

A Way Out

'Let's eat and drink! Tomorrow we may die' (v. 13, CEV).

I saiah, as God's instrument, must deliver prophecies against many nations. In this chapter, the words received are against Jerusalem. Isaiah has trouble delivering this message, for it has to do with his own people; thus, he *weeps* for them. Nothing can console him, for he sees the destruction and devastation of not only the city, but also the people themselves. They took physical precautions to prepare for an invasion; but they had neglected the most important element – remembering God through it all. It brought doom to the nation.

Battles come; and when they do, our natural response should be to get on our knees, asking for direction, strength, courage, guidance. Yet so often we forge ahead – feeling we can take them on ourselves, using our own strategy and defence tactics. Pride gets in the way and, at first, we might even think we're winning.

Then, reality sinks in. We know we've lost the battle. We might even try to put the blame on the situation itself, or on another person. The futility of it all. So, why not *eat and drink*, and pretend it doesn't matter? Drown in our sorrows. And who cares anyway?

This kind of self-pity goes nowhere. There *is* a way out. It's the swallowing of pride, admitting we're wrong. Above all, it's humbling ourselves before God, thanking him for being with us:

You, LORD, are my God! I will praise you for doing the wonderful things you had planned and promised since ancient times (25:1, CEV).

God sees from the beginning to the end. He is not only a covenant-making God, but is a covenant-*keeping* God. He has things planned, and executes gloriously his purpose for us.

Maybe today we feel 'stuck' in a certain situation that isn't going well. Or maybe someone close to us is fighting a battle on their own. There *is* a way out. God is waiting to hear from us.

Perfect Peace

You will guard him and keep him in perfect and constant peace whose mind (both its inclination and its character) is stayed on You, because he commits himself to You, leans on You, and hopes confidently in You (v. 3, AB).

We live in a world full of constant noise. Yet according to news reports, scientists have been able to achieve absolute silence. They have produced a blueprint for an 'acoustic clock' which could make objects impervious to sound waves. Outlined in the *Journal of Physics*, this new discovery could eventually be used to soundproof offices, homes or advanced concert halls.

The ability to create complete silence could definitely be an advantage in many situations. But we're not just talking about silence. Isaiah speaks of peace – *perfect* peace – even when the noise is still very much present; during times of national disaster, or even during a very personal crisis. Only God can bring perfect peace.

This passage of Scripture is really a song of praise to the Lord for his great comfort and strength, given to those who trust in him. God cares for his children, those whose mind is *stayed* and fixed on him. We have the assurance that he will never let us down.

With this peace comes an insatiable desire for God, a longing:

My soul yearns for You (O Lord) in the night, yes, my spirit within me seeks You earnestly (v. 9, AB).

From time to time, we can take our faith for granted. It's the same with relationships. The spark fades a bit, and things might become a little routine. Isaiah is saying there must be a constant *yearning* in one's heart to keep any relationship alive. A love that's to be cherished, bringing a sense of security; bringing a sense of peace.

Today, despite all the noise without and within, let's be thankful for the inner peace that's given by our loving Father. And let's pass the peace to someone else who needs God's touch upon their life.

Spiritual Awakening

The fruit of righteousness will be peace; the effect of righteousness will be quietness and confidence for ever (v. 17).

A moral and spiritual awakening needed to take place with God's people. Things were not just sliding; people were actually turning away from God, rejecting and abandoning him. The rulers and leaders were of no help, for among them there was corruption and apostasy. The prospects for God's people were not good.

Again, Isaiah brings not just a message of gloom and judgment but also one of hope – for those wanting to change their ways. A second chance for those desiring to repent and confess their sins before God. If the people would turn their hearts toward him, they would be awakened to God's genuine love for them.

With this, God was also giving to his people a promise of a coming King who would bring ultimate peace, justice and judgment upon their oppressors. They needed to turn from their rebellion; they needed to trust, and wait. If they did so, they would receive *quietness* of heart, a true *confidence* in God that would last for ever.

Many parents have children with strong wills. It starts with toddlers constantly saying, 'No!' They assert their own will, their personality; their individuality, independence. As adults, this same tendency is within us all – to be strong-willed; to really question God's will and design for us; to sometimes doubt that he even has the right answers, because we feel we have a pretty good head on our shoulders.

Being in tune with God's leading takes humility of spirit. It takes the realisation that God's righteousness will produce fruit that will last for eternity. It takes a spiritual awakening.

Prayer

Heavenly Father, with a contrite heart I ask that you will be gracious to me. How I long for you! Be my strength, morning by morning, I pray.

Short Walk to Freedom

It is for freedom that Christ has set us free (v. 1).

In his powerful book, *Long Walk to Freedom*, Nelson Mandela speaks of the inherent desire he'd always had for freedom. Although he was born free, able to run and play with other children, Mandela soon learned that his boyhood sense of freedom was an illusion. He quickly discovered that his freedom had been taken from him. Yes, he wanted freedom for himself – to be able to achieve his potential. But he also wanted freedom for his brothers and sisters, both black and white. It was to be a long walk ahead of him to gain the freedom he so desired.

The apostle Paul wanted the Galatians to be set free. Not to be bound by religious law, by rituals, by traditions; but rather to experience the freedom Christ offers to all who believe in him. Rather than our doing good works alone to gain God's favour, rather than 'playing church', not really committing oneself to God, Christ desires to liberate us all and set us free.

Martin Luther once said that a Christian is a free lord of all, subject to none; but also a perfectly dutiful servant of all, subject to all. Freedom is not what we choose, for our own gain; it's being free in Christ – to see all the potential and possibilities before us.

A Greek legend tells how Hercules instigated the Olympic Games in 776 BC after cleaning out some filthy stables – by redirecting, through his strength, two rivers. These great Greek sporting festivals were held every four years, bringing a sense of liberation, freedom, victory. It's this familiar legend to which Paul refers:

You were running a good race. Who cut in on you and kept you from obeying the truth? (v. 7).

Distractions do come. Things, people, can cause us to get off track. But it's a *short* walk to freedom, once we surrender all to Christ. It's a walk that continues and becomes easier as we grow in the likeness of our Lord and Saviour, Jesus Christ.

Fruit of the Spirit – Love

But the fruit of the Spirit is love, joy, peace, patience, kindness, goodness, faithfulness, gentleness and self-control (vv. 22, 23).

What is the Spirit life all about? Sometimes certain people think it's all about belief. As long as you believe, all will be well. But belief is strongly linked to behaviour. If we believe Christ died for us and rose again to live within us through the Holy Spirit, it introduces us to vast possibilities of unique behaviour. Paul united the idea of fruit with the indwelling life of Christ through the Spirit in his term 'the fruit of the Spirit'. He then described the fruit in more detail.

It's important to realise that it's 'fruit' – singular. We don't get to choose which fruit we like best or do better with. All aspects of the 'fruit' are to be desired and cultivated. The fruit of the Spirit is a composite description of behaviour that is the direct result of a relationship with Christ, who indwells his people by his Spirit. It's the Spirit life.

The fruit of the Spirit is *love*. Love comes first:

'Love the Lord your God with all your heart and with all your soul and with all your mind . . . Love your neighbour as yourself' (Matthew 22:37, 39).

To love God requires the combined activity of the heart, soul and mind. Our heart strives to comprehend him. Our soul responds to him. Our mind puts this love into action. In this way we can love ourselves. It's about selfhood, not selfishness. He created us. We are all unique. We are of worth to God. He redeemed us and called us.

When we have a correct perspective on how to love God, this translates into a proper love for our neighbour. God's love even helps us to love our enemy. It's all bound together in the Spirit life.

People need to love, and be loved. There are hurting homes, fractured relationships, broken people. Let's be agents of love. As God's love for us permeates our very being, may the beauty of his love be seen in all we say, all we do, all we are.

A Life of Integrity

Good and upright is the LORD; therefore he instructs sinners in his ways (25:8).

I t's wonderful to have the anticipation of something good to take place. We wait in expectation, and the excitement builds. In Psalm 25, God makes promises to those who keep his covenant and love him supremely. These are promises from someone we can trust, one who is *good and upright*; a God who is *loving and faithful* (v. 10). So what promises can we anticipate now – and for tomorrow?

He instructs us in his ways, guiding and teaching us if we're humble before him. He will reveal his design for our lives in order that we, as the Lord's descendants, will be prosperous. He makes his covenant known to us, protecting us from Satan as he delivers us. Indeed, he is a mighty God! But it depends upon us and the choices we make. Will we choose to live a life of integrity before him?

Psalm 26 truly answers the question with this opening declaration:

I have trusted in the LORD without wavering (v. 1).

We all make mistakes. We know for certain that David wasn't perfect. Yet when he confessed his sin, and was truly cleansed by God, he knew he could live a life of integrity – a life without condemnation before God.

Why is a life of integrity essential? The psalmist gives several reasons: for a right relationship with God; to have a character that is wholesome; to live with others according to God's plan; for living a holy life; for our future eternal inheritance.

Living a life of integrity means saying *yes* to many things that are positive and good; and it means saying *no* to things that will pull us down and eventually destroy us. To walk with integrity is an intentional inclination of the heart. What choice will we make?

My feet stand on level ground; in the great assembly I will praise the LORD (v. 12).

God's Soldier

Take your share of hardship, like a good soldier of Christ Jesus
(v. 3, NEB).

Although this song was written originally for a pageant, following the
commissioning as Salvation Army officers of the Soldiers of Christ
Session of cadets in 1962, it's still vital for today; for it embraces both the
passion for the mission of God's 'Army' and the continued faithfulness of
those who march forward in Christ's name. Having Commissioner Harry
Read's lyrics blended with Retired General John Larsson's music, the song
lives on – reaching out to a needy world:

> God's soldier marches as to war, A soldier on an alien shore,
> A soldier true, a soldier who Will keep the highest aims in view.
> God's soldier goes where sin is found; Where evil reigns, his battleground;
> A cunning foe to overthrow And strike for truth a telling blow.
>
> *(SASB 801)*

Soldiers are to be a disciplined people with 'highest aims'. We need to be
equipped: prayer; Bible study; more prayer. We go forward in God's strength.
It's not always an easy life, being a soldier. We go to where sin is found, the
battleground. We soon find Satan. But God is ever-present. With him, we
can't fail.

Although soldiers get tired, weary, discouraged, lonely, weighed down,
even burned out, the task is always before us all. Millions are out there, with
such great needs. With renewed energy, a renewed spirit, with a smile on our
face and a song in our heart, God's soldier *can*, by God's grace, 'turn the
world upside down'!

> We're going to fill, fill, fill the world with glory;
> We're going to smile, smile, smile and not frown;
> We're going to sing, sing, sing the gospel story;
> We're going to turn the world upside down.
>
> (refrain)

Celebration of Joy

. . . a highway will be there; it will be called the Way of Holiness (v. 8).

Much of Isaiah speaks to the coming vengeance of the Lord. The wicked will be destroyed. We don't like to hear or read this kind of language, but it's part of Scripture. God hates sin. But he always gives warnings. Thus, we have the word 'woe' appearing time and again. Justice and judgment are necessary outcomes. Depravity, sinfulness, wickedness cannot be tolerated.

Perhaps we've felt God saying to us, 'Woe!' because of something we've done; some unconfessed sin. God doesn't look upon sin lightly. But Isaiah doesn't leave his prophecy in a state of gloom and despair, just as God doesn't leave us groping in darkness. Despite all the 'woes' uttered, there's a wonderful promise for those who turn from their sin. There's hope. There's a celebration of joy for the redeemed:

Gladness and joy will overtake them (v. 10).

What blessings will come to Isaiah's people? Their desert land will blossom (v. 1); there will be strength for the weary (v. 3); the blind will see, the deaf will hear, the lame will walk (vv. 5, 6); there will be a highway – leading to holiness (v. 8); there will be deliverance from the enemy, from sin; and then we have the promise of heaven (v. 10).

It's no different today. We're to have a celebration of joy, for the Lord also blesses us – much like a beautiful symphonic piece of music blesses us. First movement – nature; new life; majestic! Second movement – deliverance; more subdued; beautiful. Third movement – fertility; brightness; the magnificent highway. Then the triumphant final movement – incredulous joy; celebration; redemption!

[We] will enter Zion with singing; everlasting joy will crown [our] heads (v. 10).

Comfort

Comfort, comfort my people, says your God (v. 1).

We have thought much about judgment, because of a sinful and rebellious people. We now come to the 'New Testament' part of Isaiah, where there is a proclamation of both comfort and hope.

It's a beautiful word, *comfort*. A child falls; we bring comfort. A teenager is rejected by peers; we bring comfort. We go to visit someone sick; we bring comfort. A cherished person, a loved-one dies; we go to stand by the family to bring some sense of comfort.

For Isaiah alone to declare 'comfort', after all the judgment that has taken place, would seem ludicrous – until we realise *who* is giving the comfort. The word is mentioned only twice in the first thirty-nine chapters; but from here on, it is mentioned time and again. Comfort, strength, encouragement for his people – God's people.

Psychologists tell us that most people, in order to be happy, must have love and affection. People need to be recognised and have a sense of self-esteem. True, a person's psychological needs may be met, to a point, apart from the gospel. But only through faith in Christ does one receive the longings of the human heart. People then become the object of someone's genuine, personal concern. The tender compassion of God consoles a believer's heart in time of deepest grief, giving meaning and purpose to life. Someone cares.

This brings great comfort; for God alone brings ultimate peace to his children. Comfort is to be embraced, for it's from him:

'The glory of the LORD will be revealed, and all mankind together will see it' (v. 5).

Thought

Could you bring comfort today to someone who needs encouragement, someone who needs a friend? When you pray with them, assure them of God's comforting arms of love.

Soaring

Those who hope in the LORD will renew their strength. They will soar on wings like eagles (v. 31).

A great moment in my life was when I went sky-gliding. I'm far from being brave by nature; but from time to time I like to do things that are a little crazy. The thought of gliding seemed exciting to me; so when the opportunity came, I went for it! I sat in a small glider plane, with a trained pilot behind me. Another plane took us up, up, up.

We were in the middle of the Rocky Mountains in the interior of British Columbia, Canada. A gorgeous sight, on a beautiful day. The plane in front suddenly let the cable go and we were soaring. I say soaring, because an air pocket swooped us up – then we glided. Other currents of air enabled us to soar again and again, followed by the gliding. No engine. No sound. Just free and effortless. Soaring, then gliding. As if *on wings like eagles*. And surprisingly, I had no fear. My guide was behind me.

For the people of Isaiah's day, these words of assurance were vital. God is saying in the Scripture passage that he brings *strength* to those who are weary; he brings *hope*, so that when they follow God's direction, they'll know he's with them – empowering them. When we follow his lead, we'll *soar* on wings like eagles.

This is one of my favourite passages of Scripture. Perhaps you feel the same way. It's a liberating, thrilling passage; the imagery of our spirits soaring high, in pursuit of all God has for us. No 'cable' holding us back. No noise from an engine. Rather, on wings, soaring – our Guide with us all the way.

The beauty, the strength, the power of his love. Let's not be afraid to let go and soar with him today!

Thought

Share this passage with someone who you feel really needs to *soar*. It will no doubt be a freeing and liberating experience for them.

Joy and Peace

The joy of the LORD is your strength (Nehemiah 8:10).

The fruit of the Spirit is *joy*. The Hebrew of the Old Testament and the Greek of the New Testament use different words to express joy. When David returned home after slaying Goliath he got a hero's welcome – women *singing and dancing, with joyful songs* (1 Samuel 18:6). The word used for joyful here is *simcha*, which refers to rejoicing. Another word for joy used in Acts is *masos*, which means jumping. *Rinnah* is yet another word conveying the thought of shouting for joy.

A further word used for joy is *gil*, which implies moving around in circles. This one seemed strange to me, until I thought of our family 'dance parties'. My eldest son, Joel, started these parties with his little nephews (my grandsons). He turns up the music, then says: 'Everyone dance!' The three boys, between one and two years old, beam with joy as they dance their little hearts out – dancing in little circles. You'd think they'd get so dizzy! But they're just so filled with joy – sheer abandonment.

Joy is to be part of our lives. If it's missing, something is wrong. As Beethoven shared with the world in his 'Ninth Symphony', his song of joy, we too can sing: 'Joyful, joyful, we adore thee!'

Yes, joy. But also, the fruit of the Spirit is *peace*:

May the Lord of peace himself give you peace at all times (2 Thessalonians 3:16).

Western travellers in the Middle East are greeted by the word *salaam*, or *shalom*. Both words mean 'peace'. Yet often in that area of the world there's gunfire and bombing. Augustine of Hippo, hundreds of years ago, said peace was the tranquillity of order. Even when there's grief, tragedy, pain, suffering, there can be a deep inner peace which only Christ can bring.

We can be agents of peace, as God continues to speak in and through us. Where there's strife, we can bring peace; where there's conflict, creating a peaceful atmosphere. Perfect peace.

Yes, joy and peace *with* God. Also joy and peace expressed in our day-to-day lives as we mingle and interact with one another.

Patience and Kindness

We urge you, brothers, warn those who are idle, encourage the timid, help the weak, be patient with everyone (v. 14).

The fruit of the Spirit is *patience*. This is a tough one for many people – in the big things of life, in the small things. The word used for patience is *makrothumia*, which literally means 'slow anger'. Interesting! Handling anger *slowly*. We might react, for we believe anger is always a sin. Paul encouraged believers to be angry *with* sin, and things which caused great harm; but to never allow such anger to degenerate into sin. People do express anger in their impatience, however. This kind of anger must be confessed.

Often we go through very difficult times and we may wonder, 'Why?' We must exercise patience – for God's ways are not our ways. If we want unity in the Church, we're to be humble and patient, *bearing with one another in love* (Ephesians 4:2). We're all different, unique. Personalities at times will clash. We're to be patient, just as God is patient with us. The world around us is full of frustration and *im*patience. God wants to shine through us, so people see there's something *different*, because of God's love.

The fruit of the Spirit is also *kindness*. There are some who think kindness is too time-consuming, too counter-cultural. After all, we live in a competitive world. Survival of the fittest! Some think people who show kindness are expecting something in return. Yet kindness should be a natural part of everyday life:

As God's chosen people, holy and dearly loved, clothe yourselves with compassion, kindness, humility, gentleness and patience (Colossians 3:12).

Kindness is being sympathetic, or even more so, empathetic. Kindness shows benevolence toward others; expresses generosity. There are many motivations for ministry, numerous incentives for evangelisation. But kindness usually beats them all. This is the fruit of the Spirit. This is Spirit-life.

Overcoming Fear

One thing I ask from the LORD, this only do I seek: that I may dwell in the house of the LORD all the days of my life, to gaze on the beauty of the LORD and to seek him in his temple (v. 4, TNIV).

F ear can grip us. The force of fear can be overwhelming and controlling. Hospitals are full of people who are physically sick. But they're also filled with people who suffer from a sickness of the psyche. Much of this kind of sickness is caused by fear.

King David had many life-encounters with fear. No doubt on the battlefield; but he also experienced emotional fears as he dealt with his own family situations. Absalom, his son, wanted to usurp the throne. He even disgraced his father with his concubines. There was incest. David himself caused grief by yielding to temptations.

Where does fear come from? The ancient Greek doctors had some interesting theories. They believed that people's personalities were determined by their inherent bodily fluids. They coined certain terms for this, which interestingly we still use today to determine personality types: the *phlegmatic* (excess phlegm), the *sanguine* (excess blood), the *choleric* (excess bile), the *melancholic* (excess black bile). Some personalities are more prone to fear than others; yet everyone is afraid of something. The psalmist says:

The LORD is my light and my salvation – whom shall I fear? (v. 1, TNIV).

Christ brings us freedom from all fear. And when we're able to master fear, through the empowerment of the Spirit, we can then become encouragers of those who are fearful. Our purpose in life then is clear: *to dwell in the house of the LORD*, for all our life; to *sing and make music to the LORD* (v. 6) because of his faithfulness.

We *can* overcome fear and be secure in Christ – now, and forever:

I remain confident of this: I will see the goodness of the LORD in the land of the living (v. 13, TNIV).

Here at the Cross

'You can't worship two gods at once' (v. 24, MSG).

We live in a materialistic world where money seems to rule. If you have it, you want more. If you don't have it, you need it – and some will go to extremes to get it. There's nothing inherently evil about money. But it can't be allowed to rule us. Today's Scripture passage tells us we can't serve both God and money. We make the choice; and it's to be everlasting. We're to serve God alone, and better each day.

> How can I better serve thee, Lord,
> Thou who hast done so much for me?
> Faltering and weak my labour has been;
> O that my life may tell for thee!
> (Bramwell Coles, *SASB* 488)

Our intentions are often good at the start. But many things can steer us in the wrong direction, pulling us off course. We might call them weapons of *mass distraction*. Our ears fail to hear God calling us; our motivation for doing things weakens.

> Dull are my ears to hear thy voice,
> Slow are my hands to work for thee.
> (v. 2)

Doubt can creep into our minds. We need to strengthen our faith, reaffirming our commitment. As we come before God today, the time with him is to be sacred. We're to be humbled before him, desiring to be revived, renewed. It's then that we can tell him we desire to be used by him. May he make us fit for his service.

> Here at the cross in this sacred hour,
> Here at the source of reviving power,
> Helpless indeed, I come with my need;
> Lord, for thy service, fit me I plead.
> (refrain)

Servant Songs

'Here is my servant, whom I uphold, my chosen one in whom I delight'
(v. 1).

We have in Isaiah what has come to be known as 'Servant Songs' – four songs that speak to what it is to be a *servant of the Lord*. They are there to reflect on as we consider what it means for *us* to be servants; to have servant-like qualities. To be like Jesus.

We speak much about servant-leadership in the Church. But what does this mean? It's really about being a servant of Christ and leading accordingly. For we're to perform a worldwide task of revelation to all who will hear: letting people know of the Lord's remedy for the emptiness of life. What then are we to do as Christ's servants?

His servant is to bring *justice*. This is the 'mission' of the servant. Again, in these days we speak much about social justice – and this is of utmost importance. There's so much *in*justice all around us. It often becomes so commonplace that we fail to see it. The servant of the Lord must be attentive, at all times, to justice being carried forth:

'I will put my Spirit on him and he will bring justice to the nations' (v. 1).

A servant of Christ is to be an agent of *mercy*, and is to be *faithful* – bringing to the world the affirmation that there is only one God. We live in a world where there seems to be much 'spirituality', but a lack of authentic faith in Christ. We must never water down our faith. We must never neglect to speak of Jesus. Only God, the *only* God, can bring mercy and faithfulness to the world.

Christ's servant is to always speak *truth* into people's lives, truth with grace always coming from the servant's lips. A servant's ministry is to be faithful, unfaltering, and always with the desire to remind the world that Jesus can meet its needs. If we, as his servants, do all God asks of us, he will be able to say:

'Here is my servant [add your name], . . . *my chosen one in whom I delight'*
(v. 1).

Let It Shine!

'I will also make you a light for the Gentiles, that you may bring my salvation to the ends of the earth' (v. 6).

Some scholars say the 'Servant' in these songs is only in reference to the Messiah. Others say it refers to the nation of Israel. Most, however, say there is a fluid nature of the servant concept; a corporate personality, for we're all to be servants of God.

What do we make of servanthood? Certainly, the servant image is a significant symbol throughout Scripture. Yet this same image has been degraded in modern times. Perhaps it's vital that we help to restore the servant image, to see its importance and worth – as we allow the perfect Servant, Jesus Christ, to make us like him. We're to be his servants in the world; and he has called us all by name:

Before I was born the LORD called me; from my birth he has made mention of my name (v. 1).

As Christians, we *do* want to reach out and tell others of Christ, and the transformational change he can make in their lives. But sometimes people don't want to hear about Jesus. Even family members. When we talk to them of Christ, they shut us out – and we become anxious, fearing the outcome of their eternal destiny:

But I said, 'I have laboured to no purpose; I have spent my strength in vain and for nothing' (v. 4).

Yes, we have to be sensitive; we have to know when to speak and when to be silent – allowing God's light to shine through us. But of utmost importance, the servant of the Lord is to trust God for the outcome; to have faith that the Spirit of God will convict in his own way, in his own time. The Great Commission of the Old Testament is given to us in today's verse – to be a *light* for the whole world. May we constantly be that light, helping to bring salvation to all – showing God's love, forgiveness and grace.

Listening and Obeying

He wakens me morning by morning, wakens my ear to listen like one being taught (v. 4).

This third Servant Song speaks to servanthood involving both listening and obeying. Sometimes we struggle with both concepts. We can hear – but do we *listen*? We intuitively sense God is saying something. But do we really listen to him?

Sometimes people accuse churches of being filled with people who 'do' many things, but fail to simply 'be' in God's presence. However, we can *be* what God wants us to be *in* 'doing' the various tasks to help others. It's vital that we listen attentively to God's voice, so we'll know both how to be, and what to do.

This is when obedience needs to kick in. We can learn to listen well, with time; but are we going to obey the Lord?

The Sovereign LORD has opened my ears (v. 5).

Obedience is not easy. Sometimes God asks us to do what seems to be the impossible. Not only do we feel inadequate; we have great apprehension and great fear. Probably God wouldn't be able to use us effectively if we thought we *could* do things in our own strength. This is where the grace of God comes into play. God's grace pours over us, enabling us to humble ourselves in obedience to his desired servanthood. With God's help we can move forward in obedience, for he is with us – to help and work with us:

It is the Sovereign LORD who helps me (v. 9).

Prayer

Lord, I do want to humble myself in complete servanthood, for your sake. Help me to *be* all you want me to be, and to *do* what you desire for me. Help me to always listen to your voice; and in the listening, to then be your obedient servant.

Goodness and Faithfulness

Therefore, as we have opportunity, let us do good to all people, especially to those who belong to the family of believers (v. 10).

What is *goodness?* Things can be good. Food can be good. We encourage children to be good. We can feel good. It's a common word that is used frequently. Things can also be bad. A bad piece of fruit. A child is badly behaved. We feel bad. But the Christian understanding of goodness is actually quite different. Its reality is found in *God's* goodness. God is the standard here, not humans. He sets the criteria by which we classify something as being good.

God created us and said it was 'very good'. Yet the 'very good' man and woman went on to disobey God. The Fall. Disobedience. But God still wants us to follow him. If we do this, goodness will 'follow us' all our days.

There's a need for goodness, to counter our human-centred, materialistic, broken-down world. For goodness does not come naturally. But because God is the essence of goodness, he desires us also to be good:

For the Lord is good and his love endures for ever; his faithfulness continues through all generations (Psalm 100:5).

Another fruit of the Spirit is *faithfulness*, which is not a commonly used word. Yet faithfulness is an integral part of our existence. Without it, societies would crumble, for we were made to operate on the principle of faith. Faith to believe we'll have enough air to breathe. Faith to believe people will obey traffic lights, and that a plane will stay in the air.

Faith requires faithfulness. In the Greek language, *pistis* is the word used to describe both faith and faithfulness, because they are interdependent. We start with God's faithfulness to us. Then it's up to us to exercise our faith in God, and extend it to others.

Gentleness and Self-Control

'Thus, by their fruit you will recognise them' (v. 20).

Some translations use the word *meekness* rather than *gentleness* as a fruit of the Spirit. Whether meekness or gentleness, there's great strength implied. Jesus was both gentle and meek in spirit, telling us to come to him when we're weary, when we have heavy stuff going on in our lives. For in him we'll find complete rest:

'Learn from me, for I am gentle and humble in heart, and you will find rest for your souls' (Matthew 11:29).

How can we live out this gentleness in our life?

- **Share Christ with others** As we do so, let's do it with a gentle spirit. Not with force or disrespect; but with optimism and hope.
- **Minister in a gentle way** Be an encourager. We need to fellowship with each other and be there for each other, with a gentle spirit.
- **Cultivate a gentle disposition** Demonstrate gentleness in all we say and do, in order to attract others to Christ and his mission.
- **Build wholesome relationships** Gentleness needs to be evident in all relationships – marriages, parent–child, friendships.

The final fruit of the Spirit is *self-control*. I wonder why Paul left this until the end? Because it's probably the most difficult? The American preacher and author Stuart Briscoe speaks of self-control as it relates to freedom – and staying on the right path:

Freedom is like a highway, with a ditch on each side. One ditch is called legalism and the other licentiousness. Legalism limits freedom by carefully defined structures and restrictions, licentiousness celebrates freedom and encourages the enjoyment of it to the point of excess, which eventually destroys the very thing it celebrates.[2]

To stay on the right path there needs to be a healthy balance, in order to have self-control within the boundaries of freedom in Christ.

Gentleness. Self-control. The fruit of the Spirit. Let's embrace them *all*, living them out to the full – so others will see Christ in us.

Help!

To you I call, O Lord my Rock; do not turn a deaf ear to me (v. 1).

M any of us have a lot of pride. We like to think we can figure things out on our own, rather than asking for help. We're sure we can fix our problems – as well as the problems of many others. To cry out for help is for the weak, for those who aren't self-confident; it's for those who depend upon others and are not self-sufficient. We're too proud to show our vulnerability. Yet there are times when we need to swallow our pride and cry out to God in our distress.

King David was a powerful man. The king in those days possessed supreme authority. He could have what he wanted, at any time. And yet he knew he was far from being invincible. He knew he could only reign well as king if God was on his side. He also knew he was human, and needed God's continual mercy upon him:

Hear my cry for mercy, as I call to you for help (v. 2).

As he called for help, he lifted his hands in adoration – knowing it was not all about him; rather, it was all about *the* King of all kings.

Often, the battles continue to rage around us. We're not promised easy lives. But when we know our Rock is with us, we can somehow get through it all. Then the Lord speaks. He does hear us, and he does respond. It's then that we can say:

The Lord is my strength and my shield; my heart trusts in him, and I am helped (v. 7).

It's not only a personal protection we seek. The last two verses of this psalm speak in a corporate sense. It's a plea for God to protect all, and to bless all. We're to be aware that others around the world who are reading these very words today may be going through some very difficult times, crying out for 'help'. And so we pray:

Save your people . . . be their shepherd and carry them for ever (v. 9).

Just as I Am

'Whoever comes to me I will never drive away' (v. 37).

One day in the early 1800s, a young Charlotte Elliott was visiting friends in London. She met the minister, Cesar Malan, who asked her if she was a Christian. This disturbed her. After apologising, he said it was his habit to ask people if they'd accepted Christ. Three weeks later they met again. Miss Elliott told him she'd been trying to find God, asking how it could be done. He said, 'Just come to him as you are.' Soon after, she wrote this hymn:

Just as I am, without one plea, But that thy blood was shed for me,
And that thou bid'st me come to thee, O Lamb of God, I come!
(SASB 293)

As a young man, Billy Graham walked to the altar in 1934 to accept Christ as this song was being sung. Ever since, he's used it in his great evangelistic crusades. God invites us all to come, just as we are. The world tries to deceive us into thinking we don't need Christ. Yet he still opens his arms to receive us. Verse 5 says:

Just as I am, thou wilt receive, Wilt welcome, pardon, cleanse, relieve,
Because thy promise I believe, O Lamb of God, I come!

We don't need to make everything right before coming to Christ; for his love breaks down all barriers. When we come, we're loved – for we're his.

The song concludes with these powerful words of acceptance by the Lamb of God himself:

Just as I am, thy love unknown Has broken every barrier down,
Now to be thine, yea, thine alone, O Lamb of God, I come!

The Suffering Servant

We all, like sheep, have gone astray, each of us has turned to our own way; and the LORD has laid on him the iniquity of us all (v. 6, TNIV).

The last of the Servant Songs brings us to the Suffering Servant, a difficult yet important passage to read. For it is a reminder, once again, of what Christ has done for each of us. Most scholars agree that the song begins in Isaiah 52:13 – three verses of exaltation:

See, my servant will act wisely; he will be raised and lifted up and highly exalted . . . and kings will shut their mouths because of him (vv. 13, 15).

The second stanza (another three verses, commencing in Isaiah 53) brings us to a period of rejection. Words and phrases such as *no beauty*, *despised*, *rejected by men*, *man of sorrows*, *esteemed him not* are used. From rejection we move to agony in the third stanza, as verse 5 states:

He was pierced for our transgressions, he was crushed for our iniquities.

The fourth stanza speaks of rejection once again:

He was oppressed and afflicted . . . led like a lamb to the slaughter (v. 7).

Evangelist Billy Graham is often asked what problem plagues more people than any other. His answer: 'Loneliness'. No one wants to admit they're lonely. Yet most have experienced a sense of loneliness. Ostracised, rejected. Surrounded by people, yet still lonely.

On the cross Christ felt so alone; ultimate separation from his Father; extreme forsakenness – all for you, for me. Which brings us to the closing stanza – for following suffering, comes such hope:

After the suffering of his soul, he will see the light of life (v. 11).

Come to the Waters

'Come, all you who are thirsty, come to the waters' (v. 1).

Joy Davidman was an atheist. Her only real goal in life, she admitted, was self-pleasure. Hedonism, her only religion. Her schoolmates nicknamed her 'Forbidden Joy' because of her passionate declarations that she intended to live for pleasure and pleasure only. Joy eventually became a Communist and did all she could to promote her belief.

Then something life-changing happened. In 1951 she wrote *The Longest Way Around* – an account of her conversion to Christianity. It contains her longing desire to search deeper into the mystical knowledge of God, wanting that knowledge to govern her everyday life. She sought out and finally married a great Christian, C. S. Lewis. One of Lewis's own books, *Surprised by Joy*, speaks of this wonderful woman, Joy, and expands upon the ultimate joy found in Jesus Christ.

Joy D. found joy, because there was a thirst from deep within. She needed to *come to the waters*. Isaiah speaks of this, extending the invitation to the whole world. To all – even to those *who have no money* (v. 1). It's an invitation, one could say, to have a benediction of joy placed upon one's life. The passage affirms that the Lord will have mercy; that he will pardon and forgive.

We're reminded also that the rain and snow come from above, and don't return. They come to water the earth. In a similar manner, God's word will not return void. It will prosper those who receive it.

Come to the waters, God says. Quench your thirst. For if you do:

'You will go out in joy and be led forth in peace' (v. 12).

Come to the waters. For then we'll be at one with Christ – having a permanent love-relationship established, that will last for eternity!

The Spirit of the Sovereign Lord

The Spirit of the Sovereign LORD is on me, because the LORD has anointed me to preach good news to the poor (v. 1).

When Jesus preached his first sermon in Nazareth, the text he read was the first and second verses of this chapter in Isaiah (see Luke 4:16–21). He ended by saying that this passage was fulfilled in him, therefore clearly Messianic in nature. The word 'anoint' in Greek is *Christo*; thus the origin of the title 'Christ'. The anointing didn't merely mean an induction to office, but inferred the Spirit of God resting upon the person, enabling him to do God's work. This was pre-eminently true in the person of Christ, who was indeed God.

As Christians, we too are *anointed* to do the work of God. When the Spirit of the Sovereign Lord comes upon us, we're empowered to preach *good news* to the poor. We're anointed to care for those who are broken; to bring a sense of freedom to those who have been held captive, those who have been ill-treated or abused. We, who have been anointed by the Spirit, are to help bring people from darkness into light; to help undo the evils brought about by sin and degradation. As the anointed we're to bring comfort, and even a sense of real beauty to people who have known only ashes.

I belong to The Salvation Army 614 Corps (church) in Toronto. The '614' title comes from Isaiah 61:4:

They will rebuild the ancient ruins and restore the places long devastated; they will renew the ruined cities that have been devastated for generations.

Only the Spirit of the Sovereign Lord can bring restoration to the cities, to the people living in our communities. We all have a spiritual obligation to reach out to the lost, those wandering in our cities and towns, who have no awareness of the transformational possibilities that will change their lives for ever!

New Creation

Neither circumcision nor uncircumcision means anything; what counts is a new creation (v. 15).

Paul wrote to the Galatians because they were wavering in their faith, unsure of their salvation. They weren't even sure how to grow, move on or mature. From the beginning of the letter he preached the gospel of grace and liberty, then went on to remind them of salvation by faith – given by God to believers. Finally he speaks in practical terms of what grace and freedom are all about, and how the fruit of the Spirit can be witnessed in the life of the believer. We're all set free to grow in grace and live a Spirit-filled life:

Since we live by the Spirit, let us keep in step with the Spirit (5:25).

It all speaks to a life of holiness. Not a self-centred life, but a life that is free enough to reach out beyond self. This is what holy living is all about. We become a new creation.

It's important to exercise our freedom in Christ in several ways:

- **Spiritual responsibility** A cartoon has Charlie Brown questioning Lucy: 'Why are we here on earth?' Lucy responds, 'To make others happy'; to which Charlie says, 'Then why are the *others* here?' We might ask ourselves why 'others' at times are so antagonistic. Our spiritual responsibility is for others – to 'restore' them gently (6:1).
- **Spiritual caring** We're reminded by Paul to carry one another's 'burdens' (v. 2), to look out for each other, and be practical in our caring. It takes effort; it takes time and patience to do service. We must have the holy 'want to', coming from the Spirit within.
- **Spiritual sharing** Yes, in a material sense we're to share with others. But also, we're to share wisdom and knowledge. When we share of ourselves, becoming vulnerable, God uses us in marvellous ways.

As his new creation, let's share this God-given freedom with others, making ourselves available to a world in desperate need of his love.

The Power of Prayer

. . . giving thanks to the Father, who has qualified you to share in the inheritance of the saints in the kingdom of light (v. 12).

Paul wrote most of his letters to churches he founded himself. He did not establish the church in Rome, nor did he establish the church to which this letter was written. It was probably intended for Epaphroditus. He was from Colossae and, after hearing the gospel, probably brought the good news back to his home town.

The Colossian Christians were on the verge of losing their understanding of the power by which all Christians are able to live. After hearing about this dangerous confusion of thought, Paul writes to instruct and encourage the believers – reaffirming the power and joy which can be theirs, if they believe in Christ. He begins by praying:

We pray this in order that you may live a life worthy of the Lord and may please him in every way . . . being strengthened with all power . . . joyfully giving thanks to the Father (vv. 10–12).

Prayer is beautiful. Praying for people close to us is wonderful. Praying for people we *don't* know is also extremely powerful. Paul prayed for the Colossians, even though he'd never met them, for he was concerned for their spiritual well-being. He thanked God for them, bathing them in prayer. He encouraged them, then told them the gospel was bearing fruit all over the world.

Sometimes we get restless because we don't see immediate results, following our time of prayer. Yet it's so important to be consistent in our prayers – for ourselves, our family, for others.

Prayer

Lord, at times I forget to pray for those I don't know personally. Help me to pray for *all* people, in order that everyone will receive power, strength, comfort and grace.

The Choice: Wisdom or Folly?

The fear of the LORD is the beginning of wisdom, and knowledge of the Holy One is understanding (v. 10).

Choices. They're forever before us. Some choices are insignificant – what to eat, what to wear. Many people have lots of choices; others have very few. But we *all* have the choice between going the right or wrong way; the choice between good or evil; the choice between wisdom or folly.

It seems simple. Yet most of us have made wrong choices. Some have serious implications. And if we make bad choices, there are usually consequences to face. As Robert Browning said in his poem, 'The Ring and the Book', 'Life's business being just the terrible choice.' For sometimes the choice made is heart-wrenching; a choice between life and death.

Often when we're contemplating which way to go, we need to remember who we belong to and what God would have us do. Legend tells of the beautiful Helen of Troy. When the army once returned to Greece after a battle, Helen was nowhere to be found. She was finally located in a seaport village, suffering from amnesia – living in rags, dirt and shame. Someone called out to her: 'You are Helen of Troy!' With these words, her back straightened and her royal look returned. She finally knew who she was, able to make right choices and fulfil her destiny.

We're all children of the King. And we're given the two invitations, according to today's Scripture passage. Which shall we choose – folly or wisdom? God calls us to greatness, to our eternal destiny. Let's embrace wisdom, asking God to direct and guide us all!

'If you are wise, your wisdom will reward you' (v. 12).

Prayer

O Lord, help me to respond to your gracious invitation to be wise.

Thou Art the Way

'I am the way and the truth and the life. No-one comes to the Father except through me' (v. 6).

> Thou are the way, none other dare I follow;
> Thou art the truth, and thou hast made me free;
> Thou art the life, the hope of my tomorrow;
> Thou art the Christ who died for me.
> This is my creed, that 'mid earth's sin and sorrow,
> My life may guide men unto thee.
>
> *(SASB 529)*

Archibald Wiggins was converted in the Methodist Church in the early 1900s. He later became an officer in The Salvation Army and wrote more than 250 songs (hymns). The words of this one are best set to the tune 'Finlandia'.

This tune happens to be my favourite. It's actually referred to as 'the Finlandia hymn', coming from the hymn-like section of the patriotic symphonic poem, 'Finlandia', written in 1900 by the Finnish composer, Jean Sibelius.

For me, the words of a song such as this penetrate the heart even deeper when married with music that effectively brings out the depth of what the poet is trying to convey. For the song goes on to speak of the importance of blending the physical, mental, emotional and spiritual components within us as we strive to follow Christ daily. It's then that we can bring peace to others. Sing with me, please, one of my favourite verses:

> I would bring peace to lives now torn asunder,
> Ease aching hearts with words that soothe and heal;
> I would bring peace when, breaking like the thunder,
> Men rise in war, and hatred feel.
> Peacemaker, Lord! Now I am stirred to wonder;
> O take me, and my calling seal!
>
> *(v. 3)*

New Heavens and Earth

'I am about to create new heavens and a new earth' (v. 17, NRSV).

We hear and read much about the environment these days. Most governments, in preparing their annual budgets, propose a fair amount of funding to combat past neglect and to enforce industries in helping to create a 'greener' place in which to live.

The Lord said through his prophet Isaiah that humankind's complete environment would one day be made new. The atmosphere and nature around us, yes; but also the conditions in which we live from day to day. God's continuous activity guarantees us that one day there will be a newness to everything.

Not only will there be new heavens and a new earth, there will be new memories, new joys, a new reason to live. We are told the *former things* (v. 17) will fade: sin, sorrow, grief, poverty, suffering, sickness, injustice. Redemption will bring new life. In reality, the Lord tells us to look to him, for he will give us a better life:

'Be glad and rejoice for ever in what I am creating' (v. 18, NRSV).

There will be no more weeping or crying; no more death of innocent children; no more little ones with protruding stomachs because of starvation; no more homelessness or unemployment; no more child labour or human trafficking; no more crime or abuse or war or terrorism or refugee camps or child soldiers or drug lords or political tyrants.

So, what will these new heavens and new earth look like? What can we anticipate as we look forward to being with our Lord forever? Peace . . .

'The wolf and the lamb shall feed together' (v. 25, NRSV).

Prayer

Father, may I help to bring about peace and joy and reconciliation to my world, through the empowerment of your Spirit.

Dare to be a Daniel

'Please test your servants for ten days: Give us nothing but vegetables to eat and water to drink' (v. 12).

The book of Daniel is a fascinating read. Because the Israelites had sinned, judgment was needed. For 490 (seventy times seven) years they'd failed to observe the law, stating that they were to give the land rest every seventh year. Thus, they were to be exiled for exactly seventy years. They were also exiled because of idolatry.

As we read this book, we quickly see that God uses human instruments to accomplish his will – someone like Daniel. As Babylon's armies stormed through Judah taking Jerusalem, Daniel's world crumbled around him. He and his three friends were captured and deported to Babylon. King Nebuchadnezzar was looking for choice young men to occupy important positions in Babylon, particularly in the administration of Jewish affairs. These four young men were good candidates.

But they needed to be indoctrinated into Babylonian ways. They were forced to not only learn the language of the Chaldeans, but were also supposed to *think* like Babylonians, *worship* like the Babylonians. They even changed their names, their identities. This is usually devastating for people! In recent history it's recorded: 'Albania has joined the list of countries taking away one of the most personal and private possessions of its citizens: their names.'[3]

This loss of personal identity would have been difficult for the young men; yet they kept strong in their faith, never wavering. Daniel and his friends were faithful, even eating only vegetables to stay pure in body as well as in spirit. They wouldn't compromise their love for God as they stood by their convictions.

No matter what we are facing, even today, may we remain strong in our faith and true to ourselves because of our commitment to the Lord. May we each dare to be a Daniel – in every aspect of our life.

A Dream of Destiny

'Praise be to the name of God for ever . . . He gives wisdom to the wise and knowledge to the discerning' (vv. 20, 21).

The fall of Jerusalem came in three stages. The first siege took Daniel and his three friends to Babylon. Eight years later, King Nebuchadnezzar took 10,000 more captives, including Ezekiel. Finally, in 586 BC, Nebuchadnezzar besieged the city, destroyed the temple, and reduced the Jewish community to rubble.

During his reign, the king had dreams which greatly troubled him. After one dream, he sought out sorcerers and astrologers for interpretation. Having no success, he issued a decree to put them all to death. After hearing of this, Daniel offered to interpret the king's dream for him. He was careful to tell the king that it was God alone who would reveal the mystery of this dream. In fact, it was to be a dream of destiny.

Daniel stepped forward in faith, asking for a delay in the execution of the wise men of the land. He prayed, asking his three friends to also pray for revelation. Then Daniel praised God in anticipation for what was to take place.

Do we ever rush into situations without prayerful preparation? No matter what God asks of us, we need to be in the right spiritual frame of mind before we do anything of significance for God's kingdom. When Daniel had prepared himself before God, he was ready to do the task God had for him to fulfil.

The dream of destiny was interpreted for King Nebuchadnezzar. The Medo-Persian army was to overthrow the Babylonians. This was to be followed by the rising up of the powerful Greek empire, to be followed by the great Roman Empire – taking Palestine in 63 BC.

A dream of destiny indeed! But even above this truth: a man, Daniel, who had faith to believe and trust in God implicitly. Do we trust God in *all* aspects of our life? Let's give him praise as we come before him today in prayer.

Supremacy of Christ

He is the image of the invisible God, the first-born of all creation; for in him all things were created, in heaven and on earth (vv. 15, 16, RSV).

The source of all power in the Christian life is found in Jesus Christ. This is possible because Jesus is God. Supreme. He is *the first-born.* Christ stands in relationship to all creation, just as an heir stands in relationship to a parent's property. Yet Christ is not part of the created order. He was present in the beginning with God:

He is before all things, and in him all things hold together (v. 17, RSV).

One of the continuing puzzles of science is the question of what holds the universe together. We know that everything is made of tiny atoms that consist of electrons buzzing around in a nucleus. Why doesn't the centrifugal force of those orbiting electrons cause atoms to fly apart? Scientists talk optimistically of a 'grand unified theory' that they hope will one day explain all of this; but they are still a long way from such a discovery. Even testing such a theory would require a particle accelerating machine as big as the solar system.

The only explanation is found in the person of Jesus Christ – the 'Grand Unifying Force' of the universe. All power comes from him, for he is *before all things*; and in his supremacy *all things hold together.* Christ also holds the Church together:

He is the head of the body, the church; he is the beginning, the first-born from the dead, that in everything he might be pre-eminent (v. 18, RSV).

When Paul says Christ is *the first-born from the dead* he is saying that he is the heir, the head, the Lord of all the new creation. We in turn are all part of a new body of men and women that God calls the Church. From him flows all power, and this same power can be ours – power that changes hearts and lives and attitudes, recreating from within. Christ's supremacy. Hallelujah!

Life with Christ

So then, just as you received Christ Jesus as Lord, continue to live in him, rooted and built up in him, strengthened in the faith as you were taught, and overflowing with thankfulness (vv. 6, 7).

People are often 'doers' by nature. Sometimes we feel if we're busy doing things, we're accomplishing something. If we take sick, or are diagnosed with a certain illness, often our immediate response is to keep on the move to get better, to find a cure. If we're travelling somewhere and there's a delay for some reason, we desperately try to find an alternative route. If we're waiting for an appointment, we get restless – wondering how to make use of idle time.

We can understand to a point why people don't want to be wasting time. Yet often we carry this same attitude into Christian living. We want to earn favour with God by being busy. We find it hard to wait on the Lord, for we need to do things ourselves. Sometimes this can hinder spiritual growth.

Paul is saying to the Colossians that they must live by faith, day by day. They were not to go searching for new ways of doing things; but rather, build on the faith they had and be *strengthened* by it. Others were pushing legalism. Paul reminds them that they are free and alive in Christ. This was the life they were to live as Christians.

Life with Christ meant freedom and liberty. It meant living life to the full. This fullness is in God, in Christ. The same fullness is available to all believers, but only through Christ. It's not our own efforts, it's not what we do to make things happen, it's not activities we engage ourselves in to fill time; it's Christ alone, in all his fullness – the embodiment of faith, hope, forgiveness, joy, peace, love – which is to be grasped and embraced by every believer.

This indeed is living life with Christ – to the full!

For in Christ all the fullness of the Deity lives in bodily form, and you have been given fullness in Christ, who is the head over every power and authority (vv. 9, 10).

Storms

Worship the LORD in the splendour of his holiness (29:2).

P salm 29 speaks to us out of the storm. No doubt we've all been caught in a storm – a storm with lightning and thunder, ferocious winds and gales. Often these storms of nature can be frightening. A storm itself has no voice; but it can *be* a voice: *the voice of the LORD* (v. 3) – a phrase that is repeated seven times in this psalm.

God is powerful, omnipotent. And when the storms come, we need to stop and realise who God is. We need to pause, acknowledging God in all his majesty and *splendour*. In the midst of any storm that arises, we need to stand with outstretched arms to acknowledge him:

Ascribe to the LORD the glory due to his name (v. 2).

When we do this, then we'll be on guard when the tempests come and the storms seem to pull us in all directions. If we stand firmly in his presence, we'll be assured of his *strength* and his ever-present *peace* (v. 11). We can thank God; yes, even for the storms.

In Psalm 30 we read of David's storm – illness. But now he has recovered. Most of us do pray when we're ill. But do we always give praise when we recover?

I will exalt you, O LORD, for you lifted me out of the depths (30:1).

We don't really want the storms. However, when they do come, we see God at work in our lives – and we're changed for ever. Our faith is strengthened; our love for God expands. For we know he's with us and will never, ever abandon us. As the psalmist says:

You turned my wailing into dancing (v. 11).

When the storms come, may they eventually be turned into dancing and joy as we acknowledge our Lord and Saviour for who he is.

God's Love is Wonderful!

Because of his great love for us, God, who is rich in mercy, made us alive in Christ even when we were dead in transgressions – it is by grace you have been saved (vv. 4, 5).

Everyone has the innate desire to love and be loved. When truly loved, nothing can really compare. This hymn by Sidney Cox, who became an independent evangelist in North America, speaks of God's wonderful, incomprehensible love for us:

> God's love to me is wonderful, That he should deign to hear
> The faintest whisper of my heart, Wipe from eyes the tear;
> And though I cannot comprehend Such love, so great, so deep,
> In his strong hands my soul I trust, He will not fail to keep.
>
> (*SASB* 48)

It's hard to fathom the Creator of the universe loving us as he does. To hold us when we have doubts; to calm us when we have fears. He brings us freedom – as we listen to 'the music of his voice':

> His love has banished every fear, In freedom I rejoice,
> And with my quickened ears I hear The music of his voice.
>
> (v. 2)

We can't begin to measure how much God loves us. Yet he lights the way, wanting to have daily fellowship with us. What does he ask in return? Only that we love him and serve him:

> My Father doth not ask that I Great gifts on him bestow,
> But only that I love him too, And serve him here below.
>
> (v. 3)

God's love *is* wonderful!

Bow or Burn

Then Nebuchadnezzar said, 'Praise be to the God of Shadrach, Meshach and Abednego . . . They trusted in him . . . and were willing to give up their lives rather than serve or worship any god except their own God' (v. 28).

I n the opening verse of Daniel 3 we are told King Nebuchadnezzar had made an image of gold. It was erected in the plain of Dura. Dura, a common word still used in the Mesopotamian region today, simply refers to a 'walled place'. Six miles south of ancient Babylon, there's a location named Dura where archaeologists have identified a large brick construction – no doubt a base for this ancient statue.

On the appointed day all the Babylonian officials, including the three young Jewish men, were gathered in the plain of Dura – gazing at the towering golden image. They were all to bow at the sound of the music, or burn to death in a fiery furnace. The three young men refused. For their belief was in God alone.

Because of this, they were charged and immediately arrested. They told the king they were willing to die for their faith; but they also believed that, somehow, God would deliver them:

'If we are thrown into the blazing furnace, the God we serve is able to save us from it, and he will rescue us from your hand, O king' (v. 17).

Nebuchadnezzar ordered that the furnace be heated seven times hotter, the three men bound, then thrown to their destiny. We know the outcome. A fourth 'man' appeared with them in the furnace. They were saved – unharmed.

People, society, culture would have us 'bow' to things that are not of God: compromises; temptations; things that can allure us. Will we remain strong and faithful, because of our love for God? Will we be courageous, refusing to give in to things that will harm and destroy us? May it be so for each of us. And may we encourage others to stay true to their convictions, holding firmly to their faith.

Writing on the Wall

'But you his son, O Belshazzar, have not humbled yourself' (v. 22).

King Nebuchadnezzar had another dream. When Daniel was again summoned to interpret it, he was terrified – for the interpretation revealed the king's humiliation and final downfall. Once dethroned, Belshazzar became the reigning king. But Babylon was facing a crisis for survival because of the Persian armies surrounding the city. The people were terrified.

To ease the tension, Belshazzar decided to host a magnificent banquet, even commanding that the sacred vessels, once brought from Jerusalem to Babylon by Nebuchadnezzar, be used as drinking cups. The wine flowed freely, and the women danced with no inhibitions.

God was not pleased. He interrupted the boisterous banquet with a revealing message of doom. Fingers of a man's hand suddenly began to write something on the wall. Belshazzar's feast came to a sudden and abrupt halt. The inscription was as follows:

MENE, MENE, TEKEL, PARSIN *(v. 25).*

The queen mother summoned Daniel once again. He delivered the message to the king, telling him that the king had been 'weighed' in the 'balance' and found wanting. He'd not worshipped God; thus his kingdom would soon be taken over by the Medes and Persians.

That night Belshazzar was slain, and Darius the Mede took the throne and kingdom. It was the ultimate fall of the Babylonian Empire. Although the king had been powerful and rich, without God in his life he was nothing. The writing was on the wall.

Prayer

O God, Father of Daniel and so many other faithful followers of the past, help me to stay true to you, never wavering in my faith. Give me courage and strength each day to be your disciple.

Taming Lions

Daniel answered, 'O king, live for ever! My God sent his angel, and he shut the mouths of the lions. They have not hurt me, because I was found innocent in his sight' (vv. 21, 22).

In the western world today there is great material abundance. Yet with it come many repercussions – such as fractured and dysfunctional family life, high rates of both divorce and suicide, and all forms of abuse. More than thirty years ago, an unsigned editorial of a well-known American financial magazine, *Fortune*, commented:

> All of these phenomena are related in one way or another to a single underlying condition – the loss of what might be called the invisible means of support, the inner resources that in earlier generations lent purpose to people's lives, connected them to the social order, restrained their conduct, and helped sustain them in adversity.

The story of Daniel in the lions' den tells us of a man who had that 'invisible means of support', giving his life purpose and meaning, shaping his conduct, sustaining him in the face of adversity. He had the secret for living; for God was at the very centre of his life.

There are 'lions' all around us – whether we live in an affluent society or not. Temptations surround us. The 'lions' seek to devour, and destroy. It's a subtle slipping away, when we begin to look elsewhere for satisfaction – even for just thirty days:

'Anyone who prays to any god or man during the next thirty days, except to you, O king, shall be thrown into the lions' den' (v. 7).

Daniel, however, was faithful to his God – in fact, praying three times a day to him. His convictions were strong; he would not compromise, even if it meant death. He loved God that much. With God's strength permeating his being, he could tame the lions that surrounded him – inside and outside of the den. Let's also be certain in our faith, so we'll remain strong. Yes, the lions will roar; but with God's power, we can and will be victorious!

Holy Relationships

Since, then, you have been raised with Christ, set your hearts on things above, where Christ is seated at the right hand of God (v. 1).

Holy living is essential for God's people. Paul tells the Colossians they are to set their minds on *things above* (v. 2) rather than earthly things. To *put to death* (v. 5) things that belong to their earthly nature. He then moves from what they shouldn't do to what they should do in order to live holy lives (vv. 12–14).

What he tells the Colossians is essential also for us today. For we're to 'clothe' ourselves with compassion, kindness, humility, gentleness and patience; forgiving one another, as Christ has forgiven us. Then most of all, we're to love one another. For when we love, we're bonded in Christ.

Paul then addresses specific relationships which are to be holy:

- **Husband–wife relationship** The key word here is *submission*. Many stumble over this passage, as well as the passage in Ephesians 5:22–33. It's important to understand that it's a mutual submission. Wives, submitting to their husbands *as is fitting in the Lord* (v. 18). Husbands, loving their wives – an *agape* love which includes appreciation, affection. It's to be a wholesome, beautiful union.
- **Parent–child relationship** Children are to be obedient. But it's important to note that parents are not to provoke or '*embitter*' their children. They're to avoid giving frustrating commands, threats that intimidate; they're not to harass them. Rather to discipline in love, respecting and loving them, with Christ at the centre.
- **Master–slave relationship** Paul spends more time on this one than the others. We might not think it's applicable in many cultures today. But sometimes we treat others as *beneath* us; we might look down on certain groups of people with pity, rather than with compassion, grace and love. We're all equal in God's eyes. Relationships with others are crucial – if people are to be won for Christ.

Let's treasure *all* relationships – as we continue to grow in our relationship with Jesus Christ daily.

Conversations

Let your conversation be always full of grace, seasoned with salt, so that you may know how to answer everyone (v. 6).

Most people enjoy being engaged in conversation with another person, or even in a group setting. There's nothing quite like having coffee or tea with friends, talking about family or work, or even about particular situations that are affecting us. In some countries people meet on the streets to talk long into the night. People long to be connected. Conversation is crucial.

But what kind of conversation? There's nothing wrong with chit-chat – talking about the weather, or the happenings of the day. But sometimes the conversations get deeper, when someone wants to share something that's on their heart. These conversations are also important and good: conversations about health, work, family – and God.

Paul tells the Colossians that they must fill their minds and hearts with things of God, in order that conversations will be pure and holy and God-pleasing.

Devote yourselves to prayer, being watchful and thankful (v. 2).

- **Prayer** Do we pray enough? All we do should be bathed in prayer, from morning to night. You have heard the phrase, 'My life is a prayer.' We might not say this verbally, for fear of possible pride or arrogance. Yet the Christian life *should* be one of continual prayer.
- **Watchful** Paul warns to be on guard against anything or anyone who could detract or turn us away from our focus on Christ. Television, mobile phones and computers can become definite distractions, even obsessions.
- **Thankful** We can never thank God enough for all he has done for us and all he's continuing to do. And when we're thankful he will open doors for us to new kinds of ministry.

Today, may all our conversations be pure and Christ-centred; for he is present, wanting to be part of all we say and do.

Prayer for Deliverance

Into your hands I commit my spirit; redeem me, O LORD, the God of truth (v. 5).

This song of David was to be set to music. So we know it was to be sung publicly. Even though it speaks to personal struggles and conflicts, they're shared by all of us in a corporate way. For all of us need deliverance.

David probably wrote it during the time of Absalom's revolt. Although most of us may not have sons who are desperately trying to usurp the throne, we all can identify with struggles and battles within, or without. Yet there's a real sense of confidence that the Lord is always with us:

Be my rock of refuge, a strong fortress to save me (v. 2).

There's a sense in which all our prayers are a testimony of confidence in God; otherwise, why pray? They're about trust in our Creator; for when we need deliverance, or protection, we know where to turn. We can 'commit our spirit' to the Lord and, in doing this, we rejoice. David exclaims in confidence:

I trust in the LORD (v. 6).

This faith, that God will deliver him and be with him, is crucial; it's a focal point on which to place the promises of God.

The road is not always easy. Trials come, often when unexpected. And some seem to have trial after trial, *as though I were dead* (v. 12). David admits that he even felt cut off, abandoned by God:

'I am cut off from your sight!' (v. 22).

Yet, deep down, David knew God was there for him. Yes, whatever we're facing, may we know that God is with us and will never leave us – because of his unconditional love.

Peace, Perfect Peace

You will keep in perfect peace those whose minds are steadfast, because they trust in you (v. 3, TNIV).

The world today yearns for peace. Can you imagine what it would be like if there was worldwide peace? It would also be an indication that even individuals within the nations would be at peace within themselves. Perfect peace.

> Peace, perfect peace, far beyond all understanding;
> Peace, perfect peace, left with us by Christ, our Lord;
> Peace, perfect peace, through eternities expanding;
> Peace, perfect peace! Peace, perfect peace!
>
> *(SASB 751)*

Some go through life, never really finding peace. When trials come, they can't find any solace. Yet we're told that at the very eye of any storm, there *is* complete calm. Christ is willing to be at the centre of all our storms; willing to bring to us a perfect sense of his peace.

> Peace, perfect peace, though the tempest round me rages;
> Peace, perfect peace, stronger than the powers of Hell;
> Peace, perfect peace, still unchanging through the ages;
> Peace, perfect peace! Peace, perfect peace!
>
> *(v. 3)*

Then when it comes to the time of death, this hymn – by Swedish composer Erik Leidzén – reassures us that God will be with us. He'll also be with us when the angels wake us, to tell us we're with Christ in glory. What peace is ours – and will be!

> Peace, perfect peace, when at last death shall o'ertake me;
> Peace, perfect peace, shall surround my lowly grave;
> Peace, perfect peace, when the songs of angels wake me;
> Peace, perfect peace! Peace, perfect peace!
>
> *(v. 4)*

Interpreter of Dreams

'The vision of the evenings and mornings that has been given to you is true, but seal up the vision, for it concerns the distant future' (8:26).

Daniel was called upon to decode dreams for both Nebuchadnezzar and Belshazzar. Then he began to have dreams and visions himself that troubled him greatly in his spirit. One was of four beasts, yet also included God as the 'Ancient of Days':

'The Ancient of Days took his seat. His clothing was as white as snow; the hair of his head was white like wool. His throne was flaming with fire . . . The court was seated, and the books were opened' (7:9, 10).

The vision recorded in Daniel 7 describes the destinies of the various nations of the world, from Daniel's time until the end of all time. In the chapters that follow, there are three more visions, all dealing with the destiny of the nation of Israel. These visions are difficult to understand and often we skip over them, leaving their interpretation to scholars. But it's important to read the entire book of Daniel; for what Daniel saw in these visions all came to pass in history.

His dreams were interpreted to him, as he requested:

While I, Daniel, was watching the vision and trying to understand it, there before me stood one who looked like a man. And I heard a man's voice from the Ulai calling, 'Gabriel, tell this man the meaning of the vision' (8:15, 16).

Daniel was so overwhelmed by being in the presence of a supernatural being that he actually fainted. When eventually he was restored to consciousness, the angel revealed the future to him, in a flash. The prophecies were fulfilled – and *continue* to be. So there's no time to waste.

Are we right with God today? Perhaps we should also ask this of others. We should never compromise our faith in Christ. It's the difference between life and death.

Prayer of Intercession

'Now, our God, hear the prayers and petitions of your servant' (v. 17).

Daniel had a heart for his people, for the nation of Israel. He identified with the people's pain and great sense of loss because of the desolation of Jerusalem, being exiled in Babylon. And so he felt the strong desire to intercede on their behalf – by fasting, then dressing in sackcloth and ashes. He begins his prayer in verses 4 and 5:

'O Lord, the great and awesome God, who keeps his covenant of love with all who love him and obey his commands, we have sinned and done wrong.'

The prayer is personal, because we must right ourselves with God before we can intercede on behalf of others. Yet it's also a corporate confession; for the people were becoming quite comfortable in Babylon, assimilating themselves into society and beginning to forget about Jerusalem. Of even deeper significance, they were beginning to forget about God. Daniel felt the strong need to claim God's promise of restoration.

The prayer itself is marked by humility, confession, worship and petition. In fact, it's one of the greatest intercessory prayers of the entire Bible.

How often do we offer prayers of intercession? Yes, we might pray for their health, or for a certain situation. But do we prostrate ourselves before God, pleading with him on their behalf? Then what about praying for our nation, our community? Daniel prayed for *all* his people. Do we pray for *all* Christians? All people?

Today let's offer intercessory prayers, beginning with confession; then asking God to strengthen, direct and comfort us all. Let's prepare ourselves; then let's *all* pray for one another, globally:

'O Lord, listen! O Lord, forgive! O Lord, hear and act! For your sake, O my God, do not delay, because your city and your people bear your Name' (v. 19).

End Times

'At that time Michael, the great prince who protects your people, will arise' (v. 1).

The last three chapters of Daniel form a unit, containing the last of the prophet's four visions. Chapters 9 and 10 describe the fate of Israel and her final sufferings under Antichrist. Behind all these prophetic details there is the constant struggle between good and evil angels, each seeking to influence the Jewish nation.

Yet even though there is great suffering, tribulation and times of struggle, there is still a message of hope for those who believe. Michael, the special angelic protector of Israel, will 'rise up'. Satan will only be allowed to do so much, before the last battle becomes final and decisive. A remnant will be protected; for in the closing days, certain Jews will come to see Christ for who he is: Messiah and Lord. When he returns in all his glory, we will know what we did to him when on Earth – and many will repent:

'They will look on me, the one they have pierced' (Zechariah 12:10).

Perhaps we don't give much thought to end times. Yes, some Jews will come to believe in Christ. This is indeed wonderful news! But what about the rest of the world? Do we know those who aren't part of the Christian family? Are we deeply concerned about their eternal fate – enough to do something about it?

Even though Christ had not yet come the first time, Daniel was told he would rise up, following his death, to one day live for ever. He was given the promise of eternal life. Today, and all the tomorrows God grants to us, let's never stop telling people of the marvellous promise of everlasting life in Christ. It will make a world of difference to them!

'You will rest, and then at the end of the days you will rise to receive your allotted inheritance' (v. 13).

What is Faith?

Righteousness from God comes through faith in Jesus Christ to all who believe (v. 22).

As human beings, like every other living being, we have the innate desire to protect our very existence by seeking out food and shelter. But, in contrast to other beings, we also have desires and concerns which are spiritual in nature – cognitive, aesthetic, social, political. They all centre around the word *faith*. For faith is an act of the personality, affecting all aspects of our personal life: faith to believe the sun will rise; faith to believe there'll be air to breathe; faith to believe in a God who loves us beyond all understanding.

When we enter the sphere of faith, we enter the sanctuary of life. For where there's faith there's the awareness of holiness, the divine:

'Do not come any closer,' God said. 'Take off your sandals, for the place where you are standing is holy ground' (Exodus 3:5).

Moses had faith to believe God had an ultimate plan for his life. It's about believing God *is*; that he's to be worshipped, loved. It's faith to believe God created us with purpose; that he wants to build a relationship with us; that he's to be the centre of our universe:

Love the LORD your God with all your heart and with all your soul and with all your strength (Deuteronomy 6:5).

Everyone wants to succeed in life. But in many cultures, success can become a god in itself – to the detriment of relationships and personal convictions. Faith is believing God defines success in a far different way from that dictated by society. It's faith to believe God works in and through us, in order that we live a holy and God-centred life. Today, let's live by faith in our Lord and Saviour:

The life I live in the body, I live by faith in the Son of God, who loved me and gave himself for me (Galatians 2:20).

The Source of Faith

The LORD had said to Abram, 'Leave your country, your people and your father's household and go to the land I will show you' (v. 1).

A bram left. He obeyed. He didn't ask *why*. He didn't ask *where*. He didn't ask *who* would be there upon arrival. He knew the *when* – for he was to leave right away. But for *what* reason? Abram didn't ask. For the patriarch knew the Source of his faith; knew him in an intimate way.

After Abram exercised faith, God made a covenant with him – then gave the promise of a child in his old age. Abram got impatient with the wait, so had a child with Sarai's handmaid (16:1–4, 15–16). But God wasn't to establish his covenant with Ishmael.

Again, Abraham believed in the Source:

'Sarah will bear you a son, and you will call him Isaac. I will establish my covenant with him as an everlasting covenant for his descendants' (17:19).

When Isaac was just a boy, God instructed Abraham to offer him as a sacrifice. He went to a mountain, bound Isaac to the altar, and took out his knife to slay him – having deep faith that the Source would give him strength to follow through. Instead, an angel called out to him, *'Abraham! . . . Do not lay a hand on the boy'* (22:11–12).

The Source of all our faith is God Almighty. We're to have a strong and personal *belief* in the Source – to the point of leaving all that's known. It's believing God can do miracles, having faith enough to trust God with our life – and the lives of those we love. This Source allows us to use words such as absolute, unconditional, infinite.

Faith is mysterious, for we can't really explain it, or even adequately define it. It transcends human understanding. Yet even a little child can exercise faith – and also have access to the Source.

May we come to God, the Source, with a renewed sense of faith this day:

Now faith is being sure of what we hope for and certain of what we do not see (Hebrews 11:1).

Faith and Doubt

'But when you pray, go into your room, close the door and pray to your Father . . . who sees what is done in secret' (v. 6).

Sometimes our focus can become blurred. Temptations are often blatantly before us. Doubts can become prevalent. And if we're not totally immersed in God's love, protection and will for our life, we can slowly lose control. The art of deception is Satan's intellectual attempt to soften our conscience. He encourages us to strive to justify dark longings of the heart through philosophising. As Christians, we want to adhere to the truth. Yet, when things pressure us, when pushed against the wall, we start to cave in.

Hedonism – pleasure for pleasure's sake – can become tantalising. Why not just seek pleasure in life? Don't we deserve it? With this kind of thinking, there comes a slight twist within our thought-life. We begin to have doubts about things, about faith. Doubts about having to adhere to God's standards:

'And lead us not into temptation' (v. 13).

Commitment is perhaps the most important moral and spiritual value, for it involves our faith. Even when pulled in a variety of directions, we hold fast to our commitment to Christ and his desire for our life. Yes, temptations come; doubts will rise up before us. Yet faith is all about keeping focused on Christ; not yielding to the deceptive voices that surround us.

Faith's about taking risks, when scepticism tries to overpower us. It's about being confident in our Lord, when confusing elements attack us from all angles. It's realising that sometimes doubt actually affirms our faith in Christ. Faith's about holding up Christ for who he is – our Lord and Saviour:

Thine, O Lord, is the greatness, and the power, and the glory, and the victory, and the majesty (1 Chronicles 29:11, KJV).

Faith and Community

They devoted themselves to the apostles' teaching and to the fellowship,
to the breaking of bread and to prayer (v. 42).

Faith is something very personal and intimate. It's our belief, what defines us as human beings; for it speaks to the core of our personality – our soul. Faith's about our spiritual self, our values, our life journey. But if we keep it to ourselves, it's not really a life of faith; for faith's to be expressed with others, in community.

Communal faith is a beautiful thing. Some say they have accepted 'faith', but have no desire to go to church or meet with others in Christian community. It's somewhat of a contradiction; for while faith is personal, it's also to be expressed with other people of like mind. It's about sharing together, fellowship, singing; it's about praying with one another:

Every day they continued to meet together (v. 46).

Jesus lived and ministered in community. At times he needed solitude and silence. But then he'd gather his twelve, and minister to the multitudes. The community is to create a safe place for people – people who sometimes come from very difficult, abusive situations. It's there to protect, enlighten, teach, encourage, strengthen one another. A faith community is often a lifeline for those drowning in the sea of despair.

Community is where people from all walks of life, diverse in every possible way, can come together and express their joy in Christ. All are together, supporting and comforting one another; they're celebrating new life in Christ as a body of believers.

When we do this, our community of faith will expand to embrace others in desperate need of Christ:

The Lord added to their number daily those who were being saved (v. 47).

What Faith is Not

We live by faith, not by sight (v. 7).

People try to define faith by putting it in a box. Some try to say faith in Christ is for the weak; used as a crutch, taking away from the intellect. Others go to the extent of saying faith in Jesus is being exclusive – saying we should embrace *all* faith groups as truth; the need to be politically correct.

Although we're to respect all beliefs and cultures, all people – no matter their faith background – and although we're never to judge others who have different faith beliefs, we must remain strong in our Christian faith. We must realise what faith is; and also realise what faith is *not*. Faith is *not* an act or knowledge. We can *believe* something is true and valid, because of various facts. Faith is about trust, about inherently sensing something *will* happen, something *will* take place. Without knowing any details, faith leaps out – embraces, in anticipation.

Faith does *not* affirm, nor does it deny, scientific knowledge. The 'scientific' knowledge of our world is tested by scholarly methods. We're glad that this takes place, and we're the better for it. But faith exists in a different realm that can't be proved nor disproved. It comes from within; a dominion that isn't tangible.

Faith does *not* imply complete fact or evidence. However, we have absolute certainty about many things in life. But faith is different – belonging to a dimension that can't be analysed or dissected. It stands on its own, and we'd be lost without it. Faith in Christ is our salvation; it's our eternal future; it's our very breath.

Faith comes from hearing the message, and the message is heard through the word of Christ (Romans 10:17).

Childlike Faith

'I praise you, Father, Lord of heaven and earth, because you have hidden these things from the wise and learned, and revealed them to little children' (v. 25).

We learn many things from our children. I'm a different person because of what my children have taught me through the years. We're blessed to have four – two daughters, two sons.

When the children were quite young, a good friend of ours became ill with cancer. Major Len Pearo, a Salvation Army officer, took quite an interest in my then four-year-old daughter, Kirsten. She'd run into his arms and they'd sit and chat. He was her hero.

When we moved, Len said goodbye to Kirsten. In the new city, every night, she prayed for him – believing God would make him better. But he went downhill quickly.

I wondered what would happen to my little girl's childlike faith if and when our friend died. So, we drove to see Len in the hospital. The cancer showed on his yellowish face. But little Kirsten jumped up on the hospital bed, totally content beside her friend.

She said, 'Major Pearo, I pray every night for you, and God's going to make you better, right?' He looked into her big brown eyes: 'I think God wants me in heaven. But when I'm there, I'm going to look down and watch you grow to be a beautiful young woman. One day, you'll be in heaven too – when it's time.'

Looking into his caring eyes she said, through her little tears, 'I'll miss you lots; but I'll be OK.' Childlike faith. And Kirsten, now a beautiful young woman, has a strong faith – very much because of her good friend, Major Pearo.

May we *all* embrace this beautiful, and reassuring, childlike faith; and may we share it with others in need of God's love.

The Art of Sharing Our Faith

Then he touched their eyes and said, 'According to your faith will it be done to you'; and their sight was restored (vv. 29, 30).

It's beautiful to claim faith for ourselves. But we're mandated to share our faith with others. This 'art' of sharing our faith is no slick programme, no sophisticated way of telling others of Jesus. Yet there *are* some things we can do to be effective and productive – as we reach out to a desperate world in need of Christ.

- **Spiritual growth** What puts a smile on your face and a fire in your heart? If the answer has something to do with your spiritual walk, you're growing in Christ – aided by the Holy Spirit.
- **Friendship** Everyone needs friends. Dr Joseph C. Aldrich speaks of lifestyle evangelism: 'Witness begins with *presence*, moves to *proclamation*, and then to *persuasion*.'[4] Friend to friend.
- **Showing love** Isaiah 58 tells us to clothe the naked, release the imprisoned, feed the hungry, care for the elderly. This is how we're to love, if we want to share our faith.
- **Speaking the gospel** The gospel is the good message of Jesus. If we have good news to share, why keep it to ourselves? We owe it to others to speak and share the good news!
- **Witnessing to the atheist and agnostic** The Russian novelist Fyodor Dostoyevsky said that not to believe in God was to be condemned to a senseless universe. Faith's not a surrender of the intellect; it's about *experiencing* God. He's a God for all people.

The art of sharing our faith involves total dependence upon God for reaching out with his love and his message. It's an adventure that is life-changing and transformational.

Living Our Faith

We have not stopped praying for you and asking God to fill you with . . .
all spiritual wisdom and understanding (v. 9).

In the Scripture reading for today, God gives to us *ten* ways we're to live our faith; what's needed to be effective witnesses for Christ:

- **Godly wisdom** – to make godly choices in life; to say the right thing; to act appropriately; to spend time in the right way; daily wisdom.
- **Spiritual understanding** – which helps us understand something of God's heart, then live according to his will.
- **Pleasing God** – by worshipping him daily; also, by treating others with respect, and demonstrating God's love on a daily basis.
- **Kindness** – in how we share the love of God with others. As we do at least one act of kindness daily, we're bearing fruit for him: *And we pray this in order that you may live a life worthy of the Lord and may please him in every way: bearing fruit in every good work* (v. 10).
- **Strength** – for God's power and strength is needed to meet the demands of the world placed upon us as his witnesses.
- **Knowing God better** – for if we want to get to know God better, we need to pray, read his Word, commune with him daily.
- **Patience** – a virtue we all need to live out our faith in a way God would have us do: *Being strengthened with all power . . . so that you might have great . . . patience, and joyfully giving thanks to the Father* (vv. 11, 12).
- **Joy** – to be joyful always; a deep joy which is beyond human understanding; a joy, even when in the midst of turmoil.
- **Thankfulness** – to give thanks to God daily, never taking anything for granted. A truly thankful heart is a demonstration of our faith.
- **Forgiveness** – even when deeply hurt. To forgive, as Christ has forgiven us: *We have redemption, the forgiveness of sins* (v. 14).

Living our faith, day by day. This is what it's all about. And as we do so, may we prove to be effective witnesses for our living God!

The Life of Faith

I have fought the good fight, I have finished the race, I have kept the faith (v. 7).

B ody, soul and spirit are not three parts of a man or woman. They are dimensions of our being that are integrated, one with the other. Similarly, faith is about the centred movement of one's personality toward something or *Someone* of ultimate meaning and significance.

The life of faith is one of passion, energised from within. It's allowing the Spirit to take control, infilling us daily. It's becoming completely vulnerable before God. It's believing in God's power to exercise faith in our life and in the lives of others.

Love and action are united in the life of faith. Faith implies love, and the expression of love *is* action. The life of faith should come naturally, in all we say and do. It's not to be secluded in a mystical solitude; but to be lived out in practical ways. It's to be part of our thought-life. The life of faith is the integration of ourselves; it's who we are. It's at the centre of our being.

The world needs people who are living a life of faith that is pleasing to God. It's all about God's light shining through us. This dark world is in *need* of God's light. The life of faith transcends religion. It's Christ *in* us, living *through* us.

At the end of the day, the life of faith is the expression of our love for God. It's being in the race of life, and keeping the faith. It's a love affair – with our Lord and Saviour, Jesus Christ.

Prayer

Father, help me to live out my faith in every aspect of my life. For the rest of my days, may I fight the good fight, finish well the race of life, and in doing this, keep the faith – for your sake.

Songs of Deliverance

Blessed is he whose transgressions are forgiven, whose sins are covered.
Blessed is the man whose sin the LORD does not count against him
(vv. 1, 2).

It's a wonderful thing to be forgiven! As a child, to hear those beautiful words: 'I forgive you' – usually followed by a hug and a wiping away of tears. As an adult, to hear words of forgiveness coming from the lips of a family member or a friend when we've hurt them – intentionally or sometimes unintentionally. It's a feeling of great relief and an opening for reconciliation.

When forgiven by God, it's almost overwhelming. We've all experienced it, for we've all sinned. When we know that we've been truly forgiven by him, we sing a song of joy and a song of deliverance; for with the forgiveness comes the reassurance that he'll protect us, helping us to avoid further temptation and sin:

You are my hiding-place; you will protect me from trouble and surround me
with songs of deliverance (v. 7).

God sees what lies ahead. It's all about God's providential care for us. The word providence comes from its Latin roots: *pro* meaning 'ahead of time' and *videntia* or *videre* meaning 'to see'. In other words, to 'see ahead of time' any potential temptation or danger; Satan's trap. Then, protecting us from being lured into something that will harm us. God wants to deliver us from evil. He wants to sing with us songs of deliverance when we triumph over temptation – with the help of his Spirit. It's about trusting God daily, for he wants to be with us every step of the way.

When we become aware of the beautiful songs of deliverance that God wants to sing *with* us, we soon realise how beautiful our relationship with him really is, if we keep true to the Lord.

Rejoice in the LORD and be glad, you righteous; sing, all you who are upright
in heart! (v. 11).

Crown Him!

His eyes are like blazing fire, and on his head are many crowns (v. 12).

In the book of Revelation we have a picture of the Lamb of God, sitting upon the throne. On his head are many crowns. The Lamb is to be worshipped by all people – and we are to crown him as the ultimate King of kings, for he is worthy. Today's hymn begins:

> Crown him with many crowns, The Lamb upon his throne;
> Hark! how the heavenly anthem drowns All music but its own.
> *(SASB 156)*

In the 1800s, tension existed between the Catholic and Anglican Churches. Matthew Bridges, who later in life converted to Catholicism, wrote six stanzas of this hymn. He wanted Catholic theology to stand firm, and to be infiltrated even into Protestant congregations. Godfrey Thring, a devout Anglican clergyman, feared Protestants singing Catholic theology; so, he decided to write six *new* verses. Most hymnals today embrace verses from both men. Verse 2, penned by Thring, opens as follows:

> Crown him the Lord of life, Who triumphed o'er the grave,
> And rose victorious in the strife For those he came to save.

It's beautiful to see how differences can come together in Christ. No matter our background, if we're totally devoted to the Lord, we're able to crown, praise and hail him *together* – now, and throughout eternity.

Bridges closes this great and majestic hymn for us. Let's sing it as our affirmation and declaration today:

> All hail, Redeemer, hail! For thou hast died for me;
> Thy praise and glory shall not fail Throughout eternity.
> *(v. 4)*

Roaring Lion

'The LORD roars from Zion and thunders from Jerusalem' (v. 2).

Externally, the northern kingdom was flourishing. A solid economy; prospering businesses. But internally, the diagnosis of the nation's condition was grave. The ten northern tribes had become indifferent to God. There was blatant idolatry, injustice, greed, hypocrisy, oppression, arrogance – all indications of a growing malignancy. Deep-seated sin.

Amos, a farmer by trade from the south, now lived in the north. He was called to be God's prophet for such a time as this – roughly 760–750 BC. The storm clouds of judgment were soon to break over God's people.

In *The Chronicles of Narnia*, C. S. Lewis portrays the Son of God as Aslan, the powerful lion. More than 2,000 years ago, the prophet Amos used this same imagery, describing God as a roaring lion – ready to leap upon his prey. Eight times in two chapters Amos also uses the expression, 'For three sins . . . even for four'. The total of seven is the prophet's way of signifying a complete and perfect multiplying of sin, deserving the fullness of God's wrath. For a holy God cannot tolerate sin and outright rebellion.

I wonder what God is saying about my city today. Or yours. Can you picture a roaring lion? Can you see the dark clouds hovering over your country, ready to pour out God's judgment upon the sin and corruption? In Amos 2:7, the prophet recounts situations where both father and son use the same prostitute, lying on garments from the poor. Perverse! Have things changed, really?

It's easy to point the finger. But what about us? Are our lives pure, blameless? Our thought-life – without blemish? Does the lion roar?

Prayer

O God, my heart aches for my community, my city, my country. I pray for wise and godly leadership. Above all, help me to live a holy life, worthy of your love and grace.

Square Watermelons

'Because I will do this to you, prepare to meet your God' (v. 12).

Farmers in Zentsuji, Japan, are in the process of preparing full-grown watermelons for shipment. These are not ordinary melons. They're square! In preparation, they were put in tempered-glass cubes while they were still growing. Why? Simply because they're much easier to store in a refrigerator. Interesting. The naturally round watermelon can become square because of the shape of the container in which it's grown.

The people of God in Amos's day were blending in with their environment; becoming complacent in their spiritual lives, fitting into the mould of the world – to the point where God said to them:

'I hate, I despise your religious feasts; I cannot stand your assemblies' (5:21).

Imagine if God were to say this about our church services today! We'd be horrified. The people in Israel wanted a religion of convenience, of compromise; a faith that allowed them to virtually do as they pleased. Church that fits into the 'containers' of the day.

It's easy to get caught up in the things of this world, the trappings of society and our post-modern culture. For instance, the Internet's a wonderful tool; but it can also bring downfall if used inappropriately. Money is important; but often the more we have, the more we want. God gave every person the ability to make lifestyle choices; but there are right and wrong choices. Choosing the wrong results in compromise – or changing 'our shape' – to fit into the world.

Square watermelons – made to *fit* into refrigerators. Conformity. Complacency. Compromise. The forces of the world are strong, exerting their influence upon us, trying desperately to *shape* us.

Let us, in response, be a transformed people. Rather than permitting the external to mould us, shape us, may we – by God's grace – be able to minister in his name, with life-changing results.

Basket of Fruit

The L*ORD* *God showed me this: a basket of summer fruit. He asked me,*
'What do you see, Amos?' (8:1, 2, HCSB).

There is nothing quite like a basket of fresh fruit ready to be eaten and
fully enjoyed. God gives to the prophet Amos this beautiful image of a
fruit basket – an apple, banana, orange, pineapple, grapes and mangos,
perhaps? Picture-perfect.

But then we read on to see that this delicious and enticing basket of fruit
will soon be utterly destroyed – all because of the nation's worthless worship.
Divine discipline is necessary, difficult as this is.

Everything can appear to look beautiful on the outside; worship can seem
to be good; people's lives can appear to look right. But if there's sin,
hypocrisy, complacency or cynicism, God cannot tolerate it. Therefore he
must, because of who he is, take action. The 'fruit' must be destroyed. It must
be replaced with new fruit – that *is* good on the inside.

The book of Amos is a book of judgment. But it doesn't leave us without
hope:

I will restore the fortunes of My people Israel. They will rebuild and occupy
ruined cities . . . make gardens and eat their produce (9:14, HCSB).

God's plan was to restore true worship – authentic worshippers. He promised
his people the restoration of the *'fallen booth of David'* (v. 11, *HCSB*); the
restoration of the house of David, coming with the resurrection of Christ –
the new heaven and new earth spoken of in Revelation 21. The *'remnant of*
Edom' (v. 12, *HCSB*) referred to the Gentiles – implying one day every knee
will bow to the Lord of lords. *All* God's children will be *'called by My name'*
(v. 12, *HCSB*).

As we eat a piece of fruit today, let's remember to pray for one another.
Please know that I'll be praying for you – asking that God will *abundantly*
bless you as you live for him, bearing fruit for his kingdom.

Sound Leadership and Doctrine

You must teach what is in accord with sound doctrine (v. 1).

Titus, a young pastor, faces the assignment of setting things in order in the church of Crete. Sound leadership is crucial for a healthy church. To be sound in knowledge of the gospel; to be sound in one's spiritual life. Also, it's important for leaders to be fully aware of doctrine, so they can have an influence upon others. For it's an understanding of salvation in the daily lives of both the leadership and the congregation itself that produces health.

Little is known about the establishment of the church on the island of Crete. We're told in Acts 2:11 that some Cretans were in Jerusalem for the Feast of Pentecost when the Holy Spirit was poured out on the apostles. They must have been among the 3,000 converts – who then went back to form the nucleus of the Cretan church. Even though the church there was no doubt small, they desired to move toward spiritual maturity.

No matter the size of the congregation numerically, its aim should be to have leaders who are mature in their faith – from the pastor to the Sunday-school teacher; from the music coordinator to the Bible-study leader. Knowledge of God's truth is more than an intellectual exercise; it's about living a godly life: people of spiritual integrity; leaders above reproach. Sound in leadership, sound in doctrine.

Few things are more important for the cause of Christ. When one's faith is sound and one's life is consistent, God then has an opportunity to accomplish his saving purpose in the world – whether on the island of Crete or right where we live at present.

Thought

Contact at least one leader in your church today – by phone, letter, or email – and let them know you are upholding them in prayer.

Practising the Gospel

This is a trustworthy saying. And I want you to stress these things, so that those who have trusted in God may be careful to devote themselves to doing what is good (v. 8).

Good works cannot save us. But we are saved to do good works. Paul's letter to Titus, to the Cretans – and subsequently to us – gives insight as to what good works we can do as Christians. It's really about practising the gospel.

We're to show integrity as we take God's Word seriously. We're to stay away from all wickedness; living lives of purity, always eager to do what's good. We're to be obedient to authority, doing good things and slandering no one. We're to create peace with others and be considerate of them. We're to devote our lives to doing good – which will profit everyone. Finally, we're to provide the daily necessities of life, in order that our lives prove to be productive:

Our people must learn to devote themselves to doing what is good, in order that they may provide for daily necessities and not live unproductive lives (v. 14).

How deep does our faith go? Perhaps the answer is found in how much we practise the gospel in the breadth of our concern for others. It's about blending theology and ethics; God's love flowing through us – as we reach out to others. For faith and life are inseparable.

Life with Christ is vastly different from life apart from Christ. It's not only about our eternal destiny; it's about the here and now. Rather than caving in to a human-centred world, we need to elevate Christ's glorious name as we interact with others.

Thought

Today, make an effort to do at least one act of kindness toward someone who doesn't know Christ. Let's practise the gospel of love.

Love Reigns

Hatred stirs up dissension, but love covers over all wrongs (v. 12).

It's my birthday today. As I get older, I'm becoming much more reflective and sentimental. So I ask that you will indulge me for these few moments, as I thank God for who he is and for loving me so deeply. For, if it weren't for him, my life would have gone in a completely different direction. But he chose me, forgave me, delivered me. I'll never be able to thank him enough:

Righteousness delivers from death (v. 2).

I thank God for my godly parents, Clarence and Dorothy Burrows – officers in the Salvation Army. They taught me to put Christ first, to trust him always. Because of their persistent prayers, I came to realise the importance of having God central in my life.

I thank God for my husband of more than thirty-six years, David. He's a man I can trust implicitly. He loves God, cares about others; and I love him more today than the day we were married. We're a team. Our partnership was God-ordained. He was made for me.

I thank God for my four children: Rochelle, Joel, Kirsten, Josh – and their beautiful spouses. They're all the light of my life. They love the Lord, and are making a difference in the world and in the lives of others. My love for them cannot be measured. They're my joy.

I've no space left to tell of my precious little grandchildren, nor my many wonderful friends. You know who you are. And so, the birthday gift I desire – more than anything else – is to celebrate this day with all of you! To celebrate the knowledge that we're *all* loved by God, more than we could ever imagine.

Together, let's take time to thank God for one another – this great family of God. May it bring deep joy to each heart this day:

The prospect of the righteous is joy (v. 28).

Amazing Grace

'My grace is sufficient for you, for my power is made perfect in weakness'
(v. 9).

This Sunday's very popular hymn has an amazing story behind it. John Newton's mother prayed daily for him after he was born in 1725, until she died when he was seven. At eleven he went away to sea with his father, later serving in the British Navy. But after he deserted, and later was found, he was chained and whipped in public.

Because of this humiliation, he abandoned all religious principles, launching into a life of sin. He soon became master of his own slave ship, bringing slaves from Africa. He treated them with great cruelty, even making them walk the plank – delighting in seeing them fall to their death into the ocean. One day a storm suddenly threatened the survival of the ship. God used this storm to shake Newton through and through. He eventually left the terrible, degrading slave trade, and gave his life to Christ – even going into the ministry. He was able to write these words:

> Amazing grace! how sweet the sound,
> That saved a wretch like me!
> I once was lost, but now am found,
> Was blind but now I see.
>
> *(SASB* 308)

Newton never stopped marvelling at God's grace – grace for a man so entrapped by such terrible sin. Precious grace. Do we treasure it? Do we leave our fears with the Lord, knowing he's with us – protecting, guarding, loving? Let's *always* praise him for the amazing grace he showers upon us daily!

> When we've been there ten thousand years,
> Bright shining as the sun,
> We've no less days to sing God's praise
> Than when we first begun.
>
> (John P. Rees, v. 4)

Lament

Because of this I will weep and wail; I will go about barefoot and naked. I will howl like a jackal and moan like an owl (v. 8).

Leaving the familiar surroundings of his rural life in Moresheth-Gath, about twenty-five miles southwest of Jerusalem, Micah journeyed to the city to deliver God's message of judgment to a corrupt and immoral Judah. The people in both Samaria and Jerusalem were using their God-given authority to cheat the poor and abuse those who were powerless. For twenty-five years, commencing in 735 BC, Micah preached three continuous themes: punishment for sin; the inevitability of judgment; then the hope of restoration – for those who truly repented of their sins.

Judah's commercial and secular culture took prominence over the worship of God. There was increasing callousness toward the weak and complete disregard for God's laws. There was bribery, corruption, abuse of power. The people wavered between faith and apostasy, abandoning their covenantal loyalty. Therefore, Micah was instructed to prophesy Judah's destruction and impending exile by the Babylonians. Things looked fairly bleak.

As Micah pronounced judgment, he lamented; he wept, wailed. In Micah 2, he lamented over the leaders; those who'd led their people astray. Yet he also spoke of hope for the faithful:

'I will surely gather all of you, O Jacob; I will surely bring together the remnant of Israel' (2:12).

We look around our cities and communities, seeing moral laxity, corruption, abuse. Do we *weep* – or has evil become commonplace? Do we *lament* over those who are lost – *wailing* over those who blatantly oppose God's standards?

Today, let's just take a few moments to *lament*. Let's bring our country before God. Then let's pray that there will be restoration; that God's light will shine once again in the hearts of his people.

In Tune with God

'But you, Bethlehem Ephrathah, though you are small among the clans of Judah, out of you will come for me . . . [a] ruler over Israel' (v. 2).

The leadership of the nation of Judah had become corrupt. They'd become morally and spiritually bankrupt. But against such a dark backdrop, God promised something for the faithful. Yes, judgment would come. But Micah was able to prophesy that a remnant would be spared – those who had remained loyal to God. And one day, out of an obscure town called Bethlehem, there would emerge a Shepherd for God's people.

King David had come from Bethlehem Ephrathah (1 Samuel 17:12) – Ephrathah being a suburb of Bethlehem. Now, from the same township, there was to come a ruler who would *shepherd his flock* (Micah 5:4). Messiah's influence would be felt worldwide:

His greatness will reach to the ends of the earth. And he will be their peace (vv. 4, 5).

Micah preached to the people that true faith comes from a heart in tune with God. But to be tuned in to him, one must lead a life that's pleasing to him. A life of purity, of holiness; sin confronted. Yet do people really want to hear about sin? Do they want to be told about their own complacency, their treatment of the marginalised in society and of those who are abused and neglected, those living on the streets?

Micah was given a tough task. We, as God's people, are also mandated to bring justice, equality and peace to all people. To be tuned in to the heart of God. For this is what true faith is all about: repentance, humility, openness, compassion, love.

Prayer

Father, in all that takes place this day, may I stay in tune with you – all you have for me, all you want me to do for and with others.

God With Us

He will bring me out into the light; I will see his righteousness (v. 9).

In the last part of Micah's prophecy, he looks beyond the coming judgment to the future day when the Lord will forgive those who are repentant. Enemies will be defeated; Israel will be rebuilt. Because of God's promise to Abraham, he will restore; for God is faithful and always keeps his promises. As he was with his people in the past, he'll be with us now – and will continue to be with us.

My eldest grandchild, Kieran Tinashe, turns four today. I was with him the day he was born, and have been so blessed to see him grow into such a sweet, loving, precious little boy. His middle name, Tinashe, comes from the African Shona language – meaning 'God with us'. He was conceived in Zimbabwe, where his parents, John and Rochelle, were serving with the Salvation Army. His name will be with him as long as he lives, just as the beautiful country of Zimbabwe will have a special place in our hearts for ever. No matter where Kieran goes in life, his middle name is imprinted on his heart, his life. God with us.

The children of Israel, difficult as it was to hear judgment pronounced upon them, also needed to hear a message of hope. They needed to know that, if they truly repented, God would forgive – delivering them from condemnation. He was with them:

You will again have compassion on us; you will tread our sins underfoot and hurl all our iniquities into the depths of the sea (v. 19).

True faith is believing – knowing! – that we can be forgiven, restored. It's knowing God is with us – then sharing this truth with others.

Thought

Make contact with someone today – letting them know you care, and that God loves them. You may be surprised by the outcome!

The Gauge for Genuine Faith

Do not merely listen to the word, and so deceive yourselves. Do what it says (1:22).

True faith and good works cannot be divorced. For faith is about taking a vital spiritual walk – indicating that God has invaded our life; then about this faith breathing in and through us, as we work for God's kingdom here on earth. This is the central message of James's letter. It's about faith that works.

It's generally accepted that James is Jesus' half-brother, the Bishop of Jerusalem, who is writing to the twelve tribes – Jews as well as Gentiles – *scattered among the nations* (1:1). He tells them, as he tells us, that we're to aim for spiritual wholeness. No matter what we face – trials, suffering, temptations – we're to remain spiritually whole, calling upon God's power to work through our faith.

Life for many is a labyrinth. As believers, we begin through the maze; yet soon hit obstacles that throw us off course, causing us to question and even doubt. The gauge for genuine faith is the ability to press on; to work through the labyrinthine difficulties we all face – constantly asking the Holy Spirit for guidance. We're to encourage others, as we engage in and embrace practical faith.

James points out that there's not to be favouritism; it's loving all equally. Then, it's doing things for people – evidence of God's love:

What good is it, my brothers, if a man claims to have faith but has no deeds? (2:14).

The Protestant faith claims salvation by faith alone – *sola fide* – and by grace alone – *sola gratia*. This is what Martin Luther and John Calvin expounded at the time of the Reformation. James would never dispute this. Yet genuine faith is also demonstrated in how we live out our faith, in practical ways. Today, may we live out our faith by doing something beautiful for someone else.

The Tongue

Likewise the tongue is a small part of the body, but it makes great boasts (v. 5).

As young children, playing at school during recess time, many of us picked up the little phrase, 'Sticks and stones may break my bones but words will never hurt me!' Not true! Words can bite, sting, plunge deep into our heart. Someone saying something hurtful can do great damage – often lasting a very long time.

The tongue can poison people, can poison relationships. The tongue can be quick to spit out harsh words that cause intense pain. And once the words are out, they can't be retrieved. Yet, destructive as it can be, the tongue can also bring refreshment, healing, encouragement, comfort:

With the tongue we praise our Lord and Father (v. 9).

We can bring such praise to God when we speak and sing. We also can build up one another with words of affirmation. Children need to be encouraged – spurring them on to be better people. Adults need to hear words of praise – not to boost their egos, but to make them better and even more productive as people. Seniors need to be told they have worth and value, so they can impart their knowledge and wisdom to younger generations.

It's so easy to spit out words that are unkind, damaging, have negative connotations. We all need to control the tongue, control our thought-life, by calling on the Holy Spirit to tame our tongue. Instead, God would have us use the tongue he has given us in lifting up his name, telling others of his love. Our tongue needs to be wholly sanctified – in order that it be used *only* for God's glory.

Thought

Throughout the day, let's pay particular attention to the words we say – to God, family, others. May they be words that honour the Lord.

Taste and See

Sing joyfully to the LORD, you righteous; it is fitting for the upright to praise him (33:1).

It's a good thing to praise God. Many do this through music. We all might not be able to play a 'harp' or a 'ten-stringed lyre' (v. 2) but all of us can sing, giving praise to the one we love so deeply.

The psalmist David is quick to tell us that we're all in this together. We're family. And since we're all God's children, we can worship together as brothers and sisters in Christ. We're connected; and so he says to us:

Glorify the LORD with me: let us exalt his name together (34:3).

David affirms God's goodness and his faithfulness, speaking from experience as our brother in the Lord. For even though he failed God, on many occasions, he was forgiven and cleansed. So, he encourages us in our walk with God; we also can be forgiven, made into a new creation. For God is good, and we can partake of this goodness:

Taste and see that the LORD is good; blessed is the man who takes refuge in him (34:8).

As we taste and see, as we listen and sense his presence, we're drawn to God by every fibre of our being. He transcends all. His beauty surpasses all earthly description. His loveliness cannot be contained in words. For he is our Redeemer, and our Friend; in him we take our refuge.

Prayer

Dear Father, help me to 'taste and see' you this day. To see your beauty in your creation, your people. To taste of your goodness, your loveliness, in all I say and do.

O Come, All Ye Faithful

Suddenly a great company of the heavenly host appeared with the angel, praising God (v. 13).

The text and tune of this wonderful Christmas carol are attributed to John F. Wade, who wrote it in Latin in the eighteenth century. He gave it the Latin name, *Adeste Fideles* – which was later translated into English by the Roman Catholic priest, Frederick Oakeley:

> O come, all ye faithful, Joyful and triumphant,
> O come ye, O come ye to Bethlehem;
> Come and behold him Born the King of angels:
> O come let us adore him, Christ the Lord!
>
> (*SASB* 85)

It's a carol about adoration; it's about the faithful, revisiting the birth of the Christ-child. The miracle and mystery of it all! The angels' response? Our response? 'Glory to God!'

> Sing, choirs of angels, Sing in exultation,
> Sing, all ye citizens of Heaven above;
> Glory to God In the highest:
> O come let us adore him, Christ the Lord!
>
> (v. 2)

Wade reminds us that '*the Word became flesh and made his dwelling among us*' (John 1:14). So, with great humility, we bow before him – Immanuel, God with us. Do you have reason to worship and adore him, to simply express your extravagant love for him today? Then please join me in singing this marvellous concluding verse:

> Yea, Lord, we greet thee, Born this happy morning;
> Jesus, to thee be glory given;
> Word of the Father, Now in flesh appearing:
> O come let us adore him, Christ the Lord!

Lukewarm

*'I will search Jerusalem with lamps and punish those who are complacent
. . . who think, "The LORD will do nothing, either good or bad"' (v. 12).*

Zephaniah, the great-great-grandson of godly Hezekiah, was also the
cousin of Josiah – the king who brought revival to God's people.
Knowing something of Israelite history, Zephaniah knew that only judgment,
repentance and change would bring restoration and new life to the nation. He
also saw that the 'revival' brought about by Josiah was not all it seemed to be
on the outside. It was only skin deep. On the inside, apathy and complacency
had set in.

The people were lukewarm. They thought they could worship, but also
live for themselves; to go through the motions without seeking God with
humble and broken hearts.

'The word of the Lord' came to Zephaniah – who was instrumental in
delivering God's message of judgment. The people had sinned. But in so
doing, they didn't really care. They didn't fear punishment. There wasn't any
anticipation of God blessing them. They just moved along, daily, with no real
purpose. But they were warned:

'The great day of the LORD is near – near and coming quickly. Listen!' (v. 14).

Have we ever been guilty of being lukewarm? We certainly recall the church
in Laodicea, seen in John's vision: *'Because you are lukewarm – neither hot
nor cold – I am about to spit you out of my mouth'* (Revelation 3:16). Pretty
graphic!

Here in Zephaniah, the repercussions of being lukewarm are no less
graphic:

'Their blood will be poured out like dust and their entrails like filth' (v. 17).

Being lukewarm in our faith is an outright affront to God. Let's make sure
we're alive in him! Let's make sure we're adhering to the Word of the Lord in
every aspect of our lives. Let's make sure we're on fire for our God – ready,
willing, to follow his lead.

Sheltered

Seek righteousness, seek humility; perhaps you will be sheltered on the day of the LORD's anger (v. 3).

In the midst of a graphic description of divine judgment, Zephaniah's name, meaning 'the Lord hides', gives an indication that the Lord *will* hide and shelter the righteous remnant. There *is* hope for those who remain faithful to him.

We still have great difficulty with passages such as today's. Rather than reading about a loving God, we are told of his anger, his wrath; we read of destruction, ruin, devastation. Yet it's important to read such passages in order to understand something of evil. We hear and read about it every day. Yet sometimes, sadly, evil becomes all too commonplace. God has given to each person the gift of free will. Many who choose *not* to love God end up doing despicable, evil things. It has been so since the beginning of time.

God *is* love, the essence of all goodness. But when people remove themselves from God by sin, they remove themselves from all goodness. There's darkness. God is all about justice. He *hates* sin, evil, rebellion. And if there's no repentance, no remorse, God speaks, then acts; for he needs to bring order to his world. This is *the word of the LORD* (v. 5).

We need to pray. What are some things we need to pray for – in order that *all* people will feel protected and sheltered?

- Those who abuse – that they'll soften their hearts.
- Those who inflict suffering – that they'll receive inner healing.
- Those who manipulate others – that they'll have changed hearts.
- Those who are power-hungry – that they'll become humbled.
- Those who victimise others – that they'll be transformed within.
- Those who rebel against God – that they'll see the light.

May God's people unite in prayer, bringing a sense of universal peace, justice and reconciliation; *sheltered* through the Holy Spirit.

Great Delight

'The LORD your God is with you, he is mighty to save' (v. 17).

Hearing and reading words of judgment is not pleasant. The various prophets of old had a tough job. But it was necessary. Zephaniah was called to deliver God's message. There were repercussions because of sin. But for those who were faithful, those who were truly repentant, there was a future:

'Then will I purify the lips of the peoples' (v. 9).

Punishment was essential. It was a harsh wake-up call for those who had been so full of pride; the arrogant and *'haughty'* (v. 11).

The prophecy of Zephaniah takes a turn in this last chapter – for God promises he'll be with those who want to serve him with a new sense of devotion and love. For those who have been afflicted by oppressors, there'll be no more affliction; for those who have been abused, the abuse will have been taken care of by God. We can then stand in his presence, soaking in these words:

'He will take great delight in you, he will quiet you with his love, he will rejoice over you with singing' (v. 17).

God – taking great *delight* in me! What a beautiful picture. Can you see God's smile over you right now? For when we take 'delight' in someone, we can't help but feel the excitement and joy welling up inside. Here we're talking about the *Creator* taking great delight in me, in you. And to add to his delight, he rejoices over us with singing. What song do you hear him singing over you? Listen . . .

Finally, God concludes by saying:

'I will bring you home' (v. 20).

Whether home on earth, or our eventual home in heaven, it's God who's bringing us. What joy; what bliss; what delight!

Thought

Throughout the day, think of God taking great delight in you; and be listening for him singing over you!

Living in the World

Don't you know that friendship with the world is hatred towards God?
(4:4)

Sometimes it's difficult, living in the world. As Christians, we want to relate to the culture that surrounds us; yet where do we draw the line? James condemns hedonism, saying it's the basis of social conflict. We all want to be happy – and the world tells us to seek pleasure for pleasure's sake. But if God's primary goal is to keep us all happy, our concept of God is all wrong. The quest for pleasure alone is an earthly approach to life – friendship with the world. There's nothing wrong with pleasure; but our goal should see beyond to what God has for us – now, and for eternity.

James says we need to submit ourselves in humility to God's grace:

'God opposes the proud but gives grace to the humble' (4:6).

With God's grace, he helps us live in the world with the assurance that he'll be with us in any time of need. Grace is the very manifestation of Christ's love for us and his generosity toward us. With him by our side, we can live and mingle in the world with an inherent knowledge that Christ reigns – wooing others to him through each one of us.

James closes his letter with a prayer of faith:

Is any one of you in trouble? He should pray. Is anyone happy? Let him sing songs of praise (5:13).

This is how we're to live in the world – by praying, by singing, by reaching out to others. It's the prayers of the faithful that will carry us from this world to the next. For *the prayer of a righteous man is powerful and effective* (v. 16).

Today, let us – by the Spirit's empowerment – be prayerful, powerful, effective witnesses for Christ, as we live in a world in desperate need of the Saviour.

Benediction

To those who have been called, who are loved by God the Father and kept by Jesus Christ: Mercy, peace and love be yours in abundance (vv. 1, 2).

Jude, the brother of James, possibly the half-brother of Jesus, tells the believers in this short epistle they're to stand firm in the truth – staying away from false teachings. He then gives three commands: *Remember* Christ's words. *Remain* in God's love. *Remove* those who speak against the truth of the gospel.

Remembering God's words is vital for Christian living. Jude tells the recipients of this letter that they're loved, called, kept. He then reminds them of Christ's words – warning of ungodly '*scoffers*' (v. 18) who would come. They were to be on guard.

Remaining in God's love is the key to life. Yes, the recipients of this letter were loved by God; but they were also 'kept' by him. We, too, are loved and kept by him. He watches over us, guarding us from attacks without and within. It's up to each of us to trust him and allow him to be Lord of our life.

Removing those who are teaching false doctrine or disturbing the peace within the church is very difficult – taking considerable wisdom and prayerful consideration. We're to give much time in prayer over this issue, calling on God's guidance before any action takes place. Jude gives wise counsel in telling all of us to build ourselves up in the faith, by the infusion of the Holy Spirit (v. 20).

He concludes by giving to us a beautiful doxology which is not simply a summary of all his words, but a blessing for all of us as we strive to live our lives for Christ. May it be *our* benediction this day:

To him who is able to keep you from falling and to present you before his glorious presence without fault and with great joy – to the only God our Saviour be glory, majesty, power and authority, through Jesus Christ our Lord, before all ages, now and for evermore! Amen (vv. 24, 25).

Priceless

My tongue will speak of your righteousness and of your praises all day long (35:28).

David experienced many emotions throughout his lifetime. Times of great excitement, achievement, victory. But also times that were very low; when he sinned, when his son turned against him, when King Saul and his enemies tried to defeat him. Psalm 35 is a cry to the Lord to bring vindication and justice. It's a cry for help, during a great time of need.

God wants us to reach out to him – at all times. To thank him when things are going well; to pour out our heart to him when things are not going well. It's interesting to see how this psalm concludes. For David doesn't say that he'll serve God *if* circumstances change, *if* things go his way. Rather, that he trusts God for the outcome – and will continue to praise him, not just once but *all day long*.

Psalm 36 continues in a similar manner. David's heart still overflows with his love for God, for he knows God is faithful – and his love is *priceless*:

How priceless is your unfailing love! (v. 7).

There are many things in life we often refer to as *priceless*: a baby's smile; an elderly person holding a child; even a faithful dog following his master. But there's *nothing* more priceless than God's unfailing love for you, for me. He would do anything for us. Indeed, Christ gave his very life so we could live with him for ever.

People are hungry to know of this priceless love. We're God's instruments who can share this good news with them, for they, too, can receive this priceless gift. And so today, let's share God's love with another. It will be a priceless moment – with possible, *wonderful*, eternal consequences.

Away in a Manger

So they hurried off and found Mary and Joseph, and the baby, who was lying in the manger (v. 16).

The beautiful Christmas carol, 'Away in a Manger', has been attributed to Martin Luther – composed for his children:

> Away in a manger, no crib for a bed,
> The little Lord Jesus laid down his sweet head;
> The stars in the bright sky looked down where he lay,
> The little Lord Jesus asleep on the hay.
>
> (*SASB* 77)

My youngest son, Josh, loved this song when he was a very little boy. He's always had a good ear for music, even from when he was two years old. He would stand and sing this song, with all the actions – tenderly 'holding' the little baby in his little arms, and 'looking' into the baby's face as he gently rocked him to sleep. You probably have similar memories of your children, or young people you know.

It's such a tender carol; so simple, yet at the same time profound:

> The cattle are lowing, the baby awakes,
> But little Lord Jesus no crying he makes.
>
> (v. 2)

Even the cows knew! I believe that, along with all of creation, they sensed something spectacular had taken place – with the birth of this little child.

The Father continues to watch over every child and adult – all because of love. In the quietness of this moment, sing softly this closing stanza, asking God's blessing upon all people:

> Be near me, Lord Jesus; I ask thee to stay
> Close by me for ever, and love me, I pray;
> Bless all the dear children in thy tender care,
> And fit us for Heaven to live with thee there.

Be Involved

They came and began work on the house of the LORD Almighty, their
God, on the twenty-fourth day of the sixth month in the second year of
King Darius (vv. 14, 15).

The prophet Haggai was born during the seventy years of captivity in
Babylon. The people had returned to Jerusalem, but were struggling
emotionally, spiritually. He challenged them to examine the way they were
living, setting new priorities pleasing to God.

Zerubbabel had started to rebuild the temple in Jerusalem, laying the
foundation. But the project stopped for sixteen years because the Samaritan
people were causing frustration for them – causing a halt to all the work. The
Jewish people were greatly discouraged – to the point where apathy set in. All
hope vanished. No repairs of the city walls; no rebuilding of the temple. There
was famine in the land, and they were still under Persian control. Everything
looked bleak.

God directed Haggai to encourage the leaders in Jerusalem to rebuild the
temple. Even King Darius approved the project, supporting it through the
royal treasury. Because of the prophet's words, the people got wind in their
sails and began to both prepare, then rebuild. They became involved,
together, as God's people.

Haggai's challenge had been to call the post-exile community of Jews
living in Jerusalem to honour God, and do his work. To set their priorities
straight. So often we get comfortable in our *religious* life, sitting back – letting
others do the work of the Lord. God wants us *all* to be involved. There's
something quite wonderful about jumping in and committing ourselves, using
the gifts God's given us for his glory.

Thought

Involvement can mean contacting people; consistently praying for someone;
caring for children of a single parent. Pray about a new kind of involvement
for yourself – that will bring honour to God.

Be Cleansed

'I will fill this house with glory,' says the LORD Almighty (v. 7).

God refers to himself as the Lord Almighty fourteen times in this short book. It reveals the power of God, no question. But it also is a reminder to us, his people, that we're to be holy; we're to be cleansed, if we're to do his work effectively. Yes, the people were encouraged to rebuild the temple. But they were reminded that they weren't building *their* temple; it was *God's* temple. We don't build *his* Church; God Almighty builds his Church, using us as his instruments.

They were to be courageous in all their efforts:

'Be strong, all you people of the land,' declares the LORD, 'and work. For I am with you,' declares the LORD Almighty (v. 4).

And if they were diligent in all their efforts, God would fill the temple with his glory:

'In this place I will grant peace,' declares the LORD Almighty (v. 9).

But before completing the rebuilding project, they were to be clean, holy. If they were entirely cleansed by God, he would bless them.

It's a daily cleansing. Each morning, it's asking God to cleanse us for the day. As we wash our faces, it's asking God to cleanse our hearts. It's cleansing so that we can be anointed to do whatever God has for us. It's the Holy Spirit, cleaning out anything that's even slightly offensive to him, making us fresh and ready and available. It's so refreshing, this cleansing that God's Spirit does in and through us. It's motivation to commence each day with God anew.

Thought

As you drink water today, as you wash your hands throughout the day, think of God's cleansing – and the significance it has for you as you live for him.

Signet Ring

The word of the LORD came to Haggai a second time on the twenty-fourth day of the month: 'Tell Zerubbabel governor of Judah that I will shake the heavens and the earth' (vv. 20, 21).

Zerubbabel was discouraged, for he had little power and few military reserves. Yet God promised him he'd be on his side – determining who would or wouldn't win the various battles. He was to be encouraged and strengthened within. God refers to Zerubbabel as *my servant* (v. 23). He wasn't an insignificant governor, but rather a key person in God's eyes – one who was obedient, faithful. Then God says something significant:

'I will make you like my signet ring, for I have chosen you,' declares the LORD Almighty (v. 23).

This promise of being like God's signet ring indicates that Zerubbabel will carry the authority to act as God's legitimate Davidic ruler. It's also an indication of hope for a *future* Davidic ruler – the promise of the Messiah.

Some people simply dream of worthy accomplishments; others stay awake and actually *do* them. Haggai's contemporaries built a temple in the midst of stiff opposition. It was their priority, the fulfilling of their dream. They moved ahead with the project under God's authority. His 'signet ring' approved all their efforts.

What does God want us to do for him? It might take some effort; it might shake us up a bit; it could be something out of our comfort zone. When God tells us we're like his signet ring, that he's chosen us, then we must be ready to respond. *Are* we ready – and willing?

Thought

Ask God what he would like you to do for him today: pray with someone; encourage a particular person; complete a certain project. Then, move on it – knowing God's with you.

Help Me, O Lord

Refrain from anger and turn from wrath; do not fret – it leads only to evil (37:8).

The psalms are rich – filled with many emotions. Psalm 37 addresses the injustices we face in life and how we're to deal with them – especially when they affect us personally. Many of us want to tackle things our own way. But it never works. God desires that we leave things with him; that we work *with* him.

Good will always prevail – even if we can't see the outcome right away. For God always triumphs. Have you ever really noticed that God, and good, are very closely related? It's all about trusting God, being fully committed to him. It's about waiting on him, and believing he will work on our behalf – and on behalf of others.

Psalm 38 further reminds us that if we want God to hear our cry for mercy and justice, we need to be righteous before him. David doesn't try to escape or avoid his sin. He knows of its depth, how it has hurt both God and others:

My heart pounds, my strength fails me; even the light has gone from my eyes (v. 10).

He speaks of his overwhelming guilt, the deception that trapped him. He speaks of slipping far away from God – and how temptation still hovers around him. But David also speaks of the strong desire to get back into a right relationship with God:

O Lord, do not forsake me; be not far from me, O my God. Come quickly to help me, O Lord my Saviour (vv. 21, 22).

Whether it's today or tomorrow, let's never be too proud or too confident that we're afraid to call out to our Lord for help. And let's call on him quickly.

Song in My Mouth

'But now, Lord, what do I look for? My hope is in you' (39:7).

The power of fear can be overwhelming. Whether it's a fear of something physically harming us, or fear of something happening that will affect us economically or psychologically, one must have courage to get through it – before the fear consumes us. Franklin D. Roosevelt, once President of the USA, said in his inaugural address in 1933 – from his wheelchair, in the midst of the Great Depression – that the only thing we have to fear is fear itself.

The psalmist David was immobilised by fear. His enemies surrounded him; and he was still emotionally paralysed, wounded, from his son Absalom's rebellion against him. It impeded him as a spiritual leader. Yet deep down, he knew he could get through it, with God's help. There *is* hope; there *is* the reality of overcoming fear. And so David cries out to God:

'Hear my prayer, O LORD' (v. 12).

Then, in Psalm 40, he declares: *He turned to me and heard my cry* (v. 1). He gives thanks to God for listening to him, delivering him, setting his feet on a secure rock: *He put a new song in my mouth, a hymn of praise to our God* (v. 3). What kind of song is in your mouth today? One of thanksgiving? Of joy? Of obedience? David's now ready to move forward, to fulfil God's will for his life. A thousand years later, Jesus himself quoted from verses 7 and 8 of Psalm 40:

'I have come to do your will, O God' (Hebrews 10:7).

Whether it's how we use our time, spend our money, or what we do with our life, our ultimate desire should be to please God. Let's sing a song from our mouth today that gives praise to the Lord!

Thirsty

Blessed is he who has regard for the weak (41:1).

Psalm 41 closes Book 1 of the Psalter. As it does, it offers a blessing for those who care for the weak. For when we think of others, God in turn watches over us. It's a beautiful cyclical motion which both encourages and motivates us. The psalmist David also says that this pleases God. When we hold our integrity, he sets us in his presence for ever. What further motivation do we need for desiring to do his will than this?

We then move into Psalm 42, into Book 2 of the Psalter, which commences with a beautiful, powerful image:

As the deer pants for streams of water, so my soul pants for you, O God (v. 1).

Thirsty. Thirsty plant life. Thirsty animals. Thirsty people – for physical water, for spiritual water. The writer speaks here out of a deep depression, desperately wanting to pull out of it. He needs the water of life to drink, to quench his soul.

Sometimes we're afraid to talk of depression; yet so many suffer from it. Good people; spiritual people. The psalmist David first had to *admit* that he was suffering from depression:

Why are you downcast, O my soul? (v. 5).

He then felt the need to cry out to God for help. Also, he needed to do some self-examination, some introspection. For God expects us to do our part toward restoration – whether it be getting medical help, confiding in a trusted friend, or other ways to bring about healing.

When we're thirsty enough, we'll want to pray, read God's Word, be patient in finding answers and receiving healing water. It will be in that discovery that we can say with the psalmist, then share with others, that our great thirst *can* be satisfied.

Come, Thou Long-Expected Jesus

'Therefore the LORD *himself will give you a sign: The virgin will be with child and will give birth to a son, and will call him Immanuel' (v. 14).*

For hundreds of years, God's people waited for the promised Messiah. When would he come? Would they recognise him? Would he set his people free, bringing release from captivity and fear? Charles Wesley captured their thoughts in this powerful hymn:

> Come, though long-expected Jesus, Born to set thy people free;
> From our fears and sins release us, Let us find our rest in thee.
>
> *(SASB 79)*

In the second verse, Wesley speaks of 'consolation', of 'hope', of 'joy'. For Jesus, Messiah, came not just for the Jewish people but for *all* nations, all those who long for freedom from captivity. He came to reign in us for ever, bringing to everyone a gracious kingdom that culminates in deliverance from all bondage and imprisonment:

> Born thy people to deliver, Born a child and yet a King,
> Born to reign in us for ever, Now thy gracious Kingdom bring.
>
> *(v. 3)*

It's up to us. If we give everything to God, relying totally upon him, one day we will be with him – praising him around his glorious throne, as this hymn's final verse states:

> By thine own eternal Spirit Rule in all our hearts alone;
> By thine all-sufficient merit Raise us to thy glorious throne.

We no longer have to wait for him. He has come, asking for our devotion to him. Let's share this news with someone today. Their Christmas will be changed – for ever!

God's Love to the World

A series for Advent by guest writer Captain Julius Omukonyi from Kenya

During the next sixteen days of Advent, Captain Omukonyi writes of how God awakens us to his truth, teaching us how best to follow his ways and serve him fearlessly. This is to be in response to his love, revealed in Jesus. To have a knowledge of God's love to the world is not enough – we must have a personal experience of it, then be willing to share it with others.

As we prepare for Christmas and joyously celebrate Christ's coming to earth, we can receive him again into our lives – Immanuel . . . God with us!

Julius Omukonyi received Jesus Christ as his personal Saviour on 25 October 1987 while at high school in Kenya. Before answering God's call to full-time ministry he worked as an accounts clerk.

Commissioned a Salvation Army officer in 1996, the captain has served as a corps officer, a youth officer, a school chaplain and administrator, and Kenya's airport chaplains coordinator. Public relations, editorial and literary appointments in Kenya preceded his transfer to International Headquarters, with Captain Omukonyi being based in Nairobi as Director of Studies at the Salvation Army Leadership Training College of Africa.

He holds bachelor degrees in psychology and theology from Kenya Methodist University.

A New Beginning

So from now on we regard no-one from a worldly point of view. Though we once regarded Christ in this way, we do so no longer (v. 16).

'It's no longer I that liveth, but Christ that liveth in me' is a chorus used many times in Salvation Army meetings around the world. This chorus can be sung and understood only by an individual who has had a personal touch from the Lord Jesus Christ. Knowing and understanding our new life in Christ means the words of this chorus – or rather, this statement – becomes a reality in our walk with the Lord. A new life, a new beginning for a child of God, is very fulfilling.

When the Lord first awakens us by his grace to receive the life he has provided for us in Jesus, we tend to comprehend the things of the Spirit through the reference base we have acquired over the years. The trouble is, we cannot grasp spiritual things through natural processes. Our lives were once concerned with the elements of this physical world, but now we realise that eternal life supersedes our momentary pilgrimage on this earth.

In Romans 12:2, Paul challenged the believers not to be conformed to this world but to be transformed by the renewing of their minds, so that they might begin to live out the life God had called them to. In today's key verse, Paul is helping us understand that this principle applies to everything. He challenges us to learn to live in a superseding reality, relating to everything and everybody from this new perspective. We can be thankful that God is the author of this renewed insight in us and he will bring it to completion.

Prayer

Thank you, Lord, for the grace that gives me spiritual sight to see things no physical eye can see. Help me to work together with you as you transform me into your likeness. May I come to grasp your light, which is the substance behind the shadows.

Being Wise

Pay attention and listen to the sayings of the wise; apply your heart to what I teach, for it is pleasing when you keep them in your heart and have all of them ready on your lips (vv. 17, 18).

What a wondrously encouraging thought that God desires to write his ways and words on our hearts in this manner. How amazing it is to think that the God we serve, the One who commands the winds and the waves and the whole universe, also commits himself to being our personal instructor and guide in all we do! We have only to apply our hearts to his instruction, to present ourselves before him as living sacrifices, holy and acceptable before the Lord (Romans 12:1). He not only takes the initiative but also promises to teach us his ways.

How do we 'apply our hearts'? We need to do our part by reading the Bible regularly, praying without ceasing and meditating on God's unchanging principles in our daily lives. Also by learning to listen to those who are wise – that is, those who know and live by God's truth and have grown in the wisdom and knowledge of God. Those we call the children of God do the will of him who created them and called them into this wonderful ministry.

Then we won't have to muster up deeper trust in God. We won't have to strive for wisdom – because, as Scripture tells us, God will teach us and lead us to a wholehearted trust in him:

So that your trust may be in the LORD, I teach you today, even you . . . teaching you true and reliable words (vv. 19, 21).

Prayer

Thank you, Father, for your desire and willingness to teach me today. You call me to rest in the fact that you take responsibility for instructing me. Plant your truth deep within me so that your name will always be on my lips. Bring me into a deeper trust in you.

No Value in Fear

When I am afraid, I will trust in you. In God, whose word I praise, in God I trust; I will not be afraid. What can mortal man do to me? (vv. 3, 4).

Have you ever found yourself in a frightening situation that has caused you to panic? Some people face that kind of fear because of a dreadful circumstance. Others may fear failure, rejection, illness or death. Children often fear the dark and want their parents to hold their hand as they walk into a dark room. I have found myself in this kind of scenario not on just one occasion but several.

When in a lonely situation, when sick in the hospital and there's no one around your bed, when in an appointment and things seem not to be going your way, it's not easy to be unafraid. When facing a lot of opposition from church members and even sometimes when given heavy responsibilities which we think are beyond our capacity, the feeling of fear puts on pressure. But once we realise that God is in control and taking care of those difficult situations, then we discover that fear has no value in our Christian lives.

When we stop running, face our Master and face our fear head on with faith, we find God. It's his presence and power that move us beyond our fears – whether they are in the past, present or into the future. We must use our Christian faith to outshine fear in our lives.

Whatever we fear, we don't have to handle it alone by working harder, trying to control things, living in denial or, worst of all, backing away from God and his promises. Instead, Scripture tells us we can turn to God when we are afraid. As we honestly admit what we're afraid of, our fear can actually draw us closer to the Lord than we ever thought possible. We're not alone.

Prayer

Lord, when anxious, I need to trust you more. Thank you for your presence with me. Please always hold my hand in the dark and frightening experiences of life. Help me to walk close to you today.

Seeking God's Approval

Am I now trying to win the approval of men, or of God? Or am I trying to please men? If I were still trying to please men, I would not be a servant of Christ (v. 10).

On many occasions, whether it's in the church or the political arena, there are people who will do everything within their reach to seek approval from others – to get certain positions in society. Different means are used to attain this kind of approval. In the communities where I have served, political leaders and even some church leaders will do anything within their reach to ascend to power.

Paul knew that if he was going to be a true servant of Christ, he could not tiptoe around the message that the people of Galatia needed to hear. They were in much danger of being led astray by false teaching, and Paul did not make apologies for his powerful words in steering them back to the truth. He knew he was dealing with life-and-death issues, because the Judaisers' perversion of the gospel of Christ was spreading like wildfire throughout Galatia. He wanted people to know that they were to please God, only. He was their only audience.

Is our focus on pleasing people or on pleasing God? What dilemmas, situations, concerns, or people do we face that tempt us not to speak out in boldness, not to live in a way that will bring God the greatest honour and glory? There is power when we humble ourselves before the Lord, for he will lift us up. Just as Paul did, we exchange being people-pleasers for a much higher calling – that of being servants of Christ! Indeed, this should be the main focus for every committed Christian.

Prayer

Jesus, teach me to serve you; to fight, and not count the cost. I don't want to be a people-pleaser. I cannot keep seeking the approval of people. I only want your approval. Help me do your will, daily.

The Son Living in Me

I have been crucified with Christ and I no longer live, but Christ lives in me. The life I live in the body, I live by faith in the Son of God, who loved me and gave himself for me (v. 20).

As we journey through Advent, thinking about the birth of our Lord Jesus Christ, the question that comes to mind is this: Is the Son of God going to find a place in my life? Perhaps you have known the frustration of trying to put your selfish nature to death. It's about as easy as putting out a fire with gasoline! In ourselves we can't destroy the old ways any more than we can make ourselves righteous. Therein lies the key. Only the living presence of the Holy Spirit *in* us can accomplish these things.

Our lives in our earthly bodies must be captured by the revelation of God's unconditional love for us, demonstrated in the life, sacrifice and resurrection of Jesus. This love is not merely a future hope. It's a present reality – now! Just as light displaces darkness, Christ in us will displace what needs to die as we focus our attention on him. He will use our circumstances to bring us to the point where we are reachable and ready to truly learn to put our trust in him. That's the time when we can begin to fight our selfish nature – through the power of Christ living in us.

As we focus our minds towards his birth, we need to create room for him in our hearts. It's true that once we lock Jesus outside our hearts and thus lack room for him, we will never please God. Christ must find a place in our hearts. We need to feed on Christ, daily. May the truth of his gospel be revealed to us as we seek his will to be done in our lives.

Prayer

O Lord, thank you for loving me and giving yourself to me. Thank you for desiring to live in and through me. May you find a place in my heart during this festive season. Help me reflect on your love.

A True Friend Indeed

Trust in him at all times, O people; pour out your hearts to him, for God is our refuge (v. 8).

On many occasions in my family, I have been amazed by how my five-year-old son William reacts when he cannot get the attention of his mum. He will resort to crying and making all sorts of noises. But we soon realise that he is only looking for a true friend who will listen to him. Everyone in life is looking for someone who can be trusted and who you can share your problems with. But did you know that Jesus Christ is the truest of friends? He is the only true friend who will never move the goalposts due to prevailing circumstances. He is the best friend anyone can have.

Today's Bible verse is an open invitation to be honest and deeply real with the Lord. It calls us to take our masks off and pour out our true thoughts and feelings to God, telling it like it is – not how we think things should be. How freeing it is to realise we can be totally honest with God and express our sadness or joy, our fears, our faults and weaknesses, our pain, desires and dreams; to know that the contents of our hearts are really safe with God, our refuge.

This same verse also reminds us that, although the specific patterns or formats for prayer are excellent principles for individual or corporate prayer times, we don't have to follow them in order for God to hear us; nor do we have to hide our negative emotions and attitudes just so we will look good. God already knows all that we are feeling and struggling with, so we can come to him just as we are and pour out our hearts to him.

He invites us to seek him daily. Just as a child will seek to get a true friend from the family, so we need to seek the true friend of every person – Jesus Christ.

Prayer

How thankful I am for the confidence and security that comforts me, Lord. Thank you for being a true friend indeed.

The Love of Christ

I pray that you, being rooted and established in love, may have power, together with all the saints, to grasp how wide and long and high and deep is the love of Christ (vv. 17, 18).

When we look at the writings of Paul to the church in Ephesus, we note that the emphasis is on living in oneness, that unity may become real in their life together. Here the church is like a body, with Christ as the head. This letter rises to great heights of expression as the writer is moved by the thought of God's grace in Christ. Everything is seen in the light of Christ's love, sacrifice, forgiveness and grace.

Indeed, this is the truth of the gospel as we approach Christmas. It's important to note that it was because of Christ's love and kindness that he decided to leave his throne in heaven and come to earth to save humankind. It's the Messiah who accepted to carry the cross and be humiliated so that he could save us from sin. This is a clear demonstration of God's love through his Son to us.

That's why, when we read today's verses, we understand that this prayer is not asking God for more head knowledge about his love but that we would *understand and comprehend it* – that it would really sink in and go from being head knowledge to heart knowledge. Most of all, it asks that we would *experience for ourselves* the love of Christ. Knowledge is not enough. It takes God's Spirit-imparting power to each of us to fathom the depth and length and width – the incomparable nature – of God's amazing love for all.

Just as Paul was praying earnestly for the Ephesian Christians, we are to ask that our roots would go down deep into the soil of God's marvellous love of Christ in our own hearts; that his love can flow through us to others. We can demonstrate his love for us as we help someone during this festive season. We have a role as God's children to show love to all regardless of our positions in society.

Prayer

During these coming days, Lord, help me to show your love to others.

The Lord's Coming

'Therefore the Lord himself will give you a sign: The virgin will be with child and will give birth to a son, and will call him Immanuel' (v. 14).

What an assurance from God himself through his prophet Isaiah to the descendants of David! This message of hope came about after Ahaz had demanded a sign. In our world today, we are surrounded by people who are demanding signs, or putting God to the test. They question God about suffering, about tragedies. They question him about their children, their employment, their marriage, and so on.

We are faced with many challenges as people, and in particular as Christians. In fact, in one of the Salvation Army corps (churches) where I minister each Sunday, I was confronted by a member who asked: 'Captain, how come those of us committed to do God's work – visiting the sick, going for lost souls, encouraging the downhearted, supporting all the programmes – face many tribulations and are targeted by the devil?'

Those who have not declared war with Satan are already in his camp. Friends, what I mean here is that we need a Saviour to give us assurance that our battle is not in vain; but at the end, there will be a reward for those who are faithful. In today's reading, Isaiah confirms to us that those who acknowledge Jesus Christ as their personal Saviour will enjoy *'curds and honey'* (v. 15).

God had to fulfil his promise to his children by allowing his only Son to be born, to save the world. It's important to note that when the Almighty God 'comes down', he comes in a majestic way. So often, it is when we least expect to experience or hear from God that he surprises us with his presence and his voice. That is when a breakthrough in a situation happens; the darkness lifts, and we see the light. This Scripture encourages us not to lose the expectancy of his moving in our lives.

As we continue to focus on Advent, we need to acknowledge the Lord's coming and open our hearts to receive him as Messiah and King in our lives.

The Journey of Happiness

Blessed are those whose strength is in you, who have set their hearts on pilgrimage . . . For the LORD God is a sun and shield; the LORD bestows favour and honour; no good thing does he withhold from those whose walk is blameless (vv. 5, 11).

During this month Christians around the world are reflecting on the birth of Jesus Christ. It's interesting to know that as Joseph and Mary travelled, they felt like any other human beings. They were tired, and couldn't find any room in the inn. However, God changed their tiredness into happiness. Christians also can only achieve the journey of happiness if they understand the meaning of Christ's birth.

In my country, Kenya, we had striking headlines in the media, reporting on priests involved in immoral behaviour. This did not go down at all well. Happiness was not present in those churches. When sin is allowed to mature, it gives birth to shame and death.

[So Jesus once said:] 'You should not be surprised at my saying, "You must be born again"' (John 3:7).

Psalm 84 reflects a longing for the presence of God in our lives. But the psalmist knows he doesn't need to wait until heaven to find happiness. Those who have set their minds on Christ can walk each day in paths of joy and happiness. Our hope is not in a distant city with streets of gold alone. Our hope is in the omnipresent Lord God, who travels with us each step of the journey. He is the One who sheds light on our dark path and protects us from evil. His love is sufficient for us all, especially if we call on his name. Those who walk in his light and seek his will in their lives will never have regrets.

Jesus is the reason for our Christmas and we should be happy to celebrate his birth. In everything that takes place during this festive season, let's not lose sight of the One who sojourns with us. Let's acknowledge him as Lord and Saviour of our lives. Let's set our minds on our goal – our hope; then live every day strengthened in the glorious light of God's presence.

Focusing on our Future and Hope

'For I know the plans I have for you,' declares the LORD, 'plans to prosper you and not to harm you, plans to give you hope and a future. Then you will call upon me . . . and I will listen to you. You will seek me and find me when you seek me with all your heart' (vv. 11–13).

December is a special month in the Christian calendar. It's a month when hope is given to all, through the birth of Jesus Christ. Everyone wants to be given hope and the assurance that all is well. I recall how, one day, I decided to go for an HIV/Aids test with my wife, wanting to know our status. After being taken through the counselling process, we gave our blood samples and were told to wait for the results. While we waited, what was going through my mind was a message of hope. We expected all would be well, giving us hope and assurance for the future – safe from this scourge.

Everyone wants to hear the message of hope – a future that's bright. The Israelites, as we have learned from today's reading, were to be exiled to Babylon for seventy years. Their lives would be turned upside down. Yet God gave them a message of hope to guide them through their years of captivity:

'I know the plans I have for you . . . to give you hope and a future' (v. 11).

His plans for you and me were established before the foundation of the world, and nothing can derail them. So when our lives don't make sense, and our future looks hopeless, the truth in today's verses gives us a new perspective.

We must seek God earnestly; then we can expect to see his good plans for the future. May the good Lord who gives us hope and a future see us through this festive season.

Prayer

Lord, thank you that you have planned a future and given me a hope for my life. Help me to submit to your will for my future, and to have a hope grounded in your unchanging love.

God's Peace to His People

Pray for the peace of Jerusalem: 'May those who love you be secure. May there be peace within your walls and security within your citadels.' For the sake of my brothers and friends, I will say, 'Peace be within you' (vv. 6–8).

Jerusalem was once in the hands of the Jebusites, but they had been driven out. Jerusalem was now in the possession of the children of God. And so, when they made their annual pilgrimage to celebrate the different feasts, King David would sing Psalm 122 as an announcement. He wanted all the people to know that Jerusalem was the city where God would record his name.

Though David had a vested interest in Jerusalem, it was not his welfare that he solicited. He was a man of worship who loved the house of God. His desire was that God's peace and glory should come and continue to abide in Jerusalem. While we think about the coming of our Lord during this Christmas period, we can pray that his peace and glory will fill *our* hearts.

As Christmas approaches, a lot of time is spent in preparation. Traditionally, in our family this is the time to decorate the house and the Christmas tree; a time to buy presents and to send cards to our dear friends. It's also a time to visit relatives and enjoy meals together. I remember when I was young, we never ate well because I was born into a family of thirty-six children. My father was a polygamist with fifteen wives. We never had special meals. But if there ever was a time for eating, it was Christmas. There was chicken, rice, and a lovely breakfast which included chapatti – a special African doughnut. We all wanted Christmas to come quickly!

In the church, this is a time to prepare our hearts and souls for the message of Christmas. Advent – the Christian festival leading to Christmas – means 'coming' or 'arrival'. It's a time when Christians are encouraged to remember not only that Jesus came into the world in Palestine 2,000 years ago, but also that he promised to return one day in his glory. Christians should prepare their hearts for his return – his second 'coming'.

The First Love

'For God so loved the world that he gave his one and only Son, that whoever believes in him shall not perish but have eternal life' (v. 16).

Why would I want to be like Jesus? Because to be like Jesus means to be compassionate, honest, faithful, productive, morally upright, sacrificial. To be like him means to value human life, to be committed to the cause of Christ. It's all about coming into a saving knowledge of Jesus.

According to John, God loved us first in sending his Son. His love demonstrated that Jesus left his throne to come to us – to save us. First love, someone said, is abandoning all for a love that has abandoned all. It refers to such a deep devotion to Christ that we will abandon everything for the One who gave his life for us.

Maybe when you first surrendered to Christ, you couldn't wait to spend time with Jesus. You read your Bible, you prayed often. Then, perhaps, you got busy with other things and began losing the newness of being in his presence. How deep is our devotion to Jesus today?

We also welcome Christmas as a chance to give each other gifts in memory of the birth of Jesus. I remember my son receiving a pair of shoes from a leader in our church. From then on he always wanted a pair just like them that would fit. We could never seem to find the exact kind – like the ones he first fell in love with that Christmas.

This reminds me of God's love for us. He gave us the best, his only Son – a demonstration of his unlimited and unchanging love for us. This Christmas we need to give our very best to him and also remember to share something of that love with others.

Prayer

Lord, help me to abandon myself to you this Christmas. Help me to extend your love to others who are in need. Also, help me to always remember that you are my first love!

An Eternal Prophecy

For to us a child is born, to us a son is given, and the government will be on his shoulders. And he will be called Wonderful Counsellor, Mighty God, Everlasting Father, Prince of Peace. Of the increase of his government and peace there will be no end (vv. 6, 7).

When Isaiah gives his prophecy about the birth of Jesus Christ, he is very open. God reveals to him that the Lord is to be born. His qualities are defined and acknowledged. Scripture gives us both hope and certain understanding of Jesus' role.

The Word reveals the abundant life offered by the Lord Jesus today. But do we live this life? Or is our spiritual walk shattered by sin, corrupted by covetousness, wounded by worldliness? If the lost are to be brought into the kingdom of God through the birth of Jesus, then we must show them that a new birth is worth living. But they can't see Jesus in us if we are like the world around us. We must joyfully live the life that our Lord desires us to.

Isaiah was categorical in saying a child is born to us; a Son is given to us to be our Ruler, and will be our Counsellor. What an assurance we have! When we encounter problems – political, economic, moral – we have a King, a Ruler and a Counsellor who is ready to take on our concerns and share with us. God is lovely and cares for us all.

Although the book of Revelation is puzzling and beyond our understanding, it tells us that, one day, every knee will bow, and we will join the elders and the company of heaven to worship the King of kings. He is worthy to receive all glory, honour and praise.

Prayer

Lord, you are worthy of my worship! It is for you and because of you that all things exist. Give me glimpses of how infinite, limitless and majestic you are so that your glory is my focus. All that I am, I give to you.

Great News is Announced

The angel went to her and said, 'Greetings, you who are highly favoured!
The Lord is with you.' Mary was greatly troubled at his words and
wondered what kind of greeting this might be. But the angel said to her,
'Do not be afraid, Mary, you have found favour with God' (vv. 28–30).

What a chance for Mary – to be the mother of Jesus! A faithful, obedient, honest, straightforward young lady in the eyes of God. Angel Gabriel had great news for this God-fearing girl. The news was confirming God's miraculous ways in Mary's life, for when we walk with the Lord in the light of his word, he will accomplish all the plans he has in store for us.

Gabriel brought good news to Mary in regard to the birth of the Lord Jesus Christ. God defined the role of the child who was to be born. He would be called Jesus, the Son of the Most High God. He would be King of a kingdom that would never end.

The true meaning of Christmas is the celebration of this incredible act of love. It's about God coming in the Person of Jesus. Why did God do this? Because he loves us! Why is Christmas necessary? Because we need the Saviour! Why does God love us so much? Because he *is* love! Why do we celebrate Christmas? Out of gratitude for what God's done for us.

We remember Jesus' birth by giving gifts, worshipping, by being conscious of the less fortunate – because the true meaning of Christmas is love. God loved his own, and provided a way – the only way – for us to spend eternity with him. He gave his only Son to take our punishment for our sins. He paid the price in full, and we are free from condemnation when we accept that free gift of love.

Prayer

Lord, you are not interested in an outward show or performance, in elaborate sacrifices or religious acts. You want to develop in us the heart responses of humility, mercy, love and justice. Teach me to be humble like Mary, so you can work through me.

The Joy of Jesus' Birth

But the angel said to them, 'Do not be afraid. I bring you good news of great joy that will be for all the people' (v. 10).

Christmas joy, for me, is a season, a happening, an experience. It's like a long story, a big book highlighting the account of Jesus' birth. Christmas joy starts when December draws closer every year. The Christmas music, the decorations, the choir practices in church.

In Kenya during the month of December it's our summer time and the skies are clear. Almost everyone becomes generous and kind in their talk. There are lots of promises of going upcountry, or those in rural areas getting invitations from their beloved husbands or parents to visit them in the cities.

Christmas joy mostly begins in early December as everyone has great expectations leading to a glorious Christmas Day. What encourages me is that we're all in this *together* around the world. And here in Kenya it's about us, as a country, living through Christmas as people of God.

All these preparations are wonderful – and we certainly appreciate what we receive from others. But what is the real meaning of Christmas? Luke gives us an interesting account about the Lord's coming and the need to be joyous as we plan to celebrate. Jesus is willing to come and live among us. He is the reason for this season.

We live in a world that offers no end of 'things' as sources of satisfaction and happiness. But they will never satisfy our real longings. Without God, we will always come up empty because he designed us for communion with him and he alone can fill our emptiness. Only the soul that has experienced intimate oneness with the Creator will know true fulfilment.

Prayer

Lord, open my heart to spiritually perceive your truth. Help me to understand the true joy of Christmas, and help me to pass on the joy of this season to someone around me.

Jesus Christ is Born

She gave birth to her firstborn, a son. She wrapped him in cloths and placed him in a manger, because there was no room for them in the inn (v. 7).

It was about to happen – the baby was to be born. Joseph was amazed when Mary called out to him, saying it was time. When he looked at her, he felt so proud. Even though she was so tired, she was so beautiful. He wondered where he could get a room for them, for the town was crowded. There was no place for them in the inn.

The sun had fallen and the chilly night breeze cut through their robes. They were tired, hungry, and a long way from home. They simply had to find somewhere – quickly! There was only one place they could go, really. An innkeeper said he had some stables. It's all he had to give them – and there would be no charge. Actually, it was a little cave cut into the hillside behind the inn. It was rather dark, and smelly. But at least there was room to lie down in the midst of dirt and straw. It was certainly better than nothing.

The moment arrived. Mary cried out in pain. Then suddenly, a tiny sound. It was a boy; a beautiful, healthy, brand-spanking-new baby boy. His name was to be called Immanuel – 'God with us'. What an experience for a young couple! It was in God's plan that the Messiah would be born in Bethlehem, from a humble beginning.

We must all create room for Jesus again this Christmas Day. He is the King of kings, the Wonderful Counsellor, the Lord of lords, the Prince of Peace. He is our Saviour, Jesus Christ. Be blessed as you ponder on the birth of our Lord Jesus Christ today.

Prayer

Lord, I thank you for the gift of your only Son, Jesus Christ. I want to restore my relationship with him this Christmas. Help me to acknowledge him as Saviour in my life – today and for ever.

Post-Christmas Gift

Send Your light and Your truth; let them lead me (v. 3, HCSB).

We have just experienced another Christmas. I pray it was a wonderful time for you, your family, your friends! Yet for some, it was no doubt a difficult time; perhaps family members who had died were not present around the dinner table. For others who have had a tough year, Christmas may have brought tears of sadness with various memories of disappointment and discouragement.

Whether you knew joy or particular sorrow, I pray you had a fresh glimpse of the newborn babe – our Saviour, our Lord, God Incarnate! And although it's soon time to put 'decorations' away, to stop singing the beautiful carols, to take the lights down, to bring a halt to the festivities, we're to realise that this is the time when 'Christmas' really begins – as we look to a world in desperate need of God's love.

The psalmist David asked for two things, two gifts: truth and light. He wanted God's Word implanted in his heart – the *truth*. Then he wanted understanding of it – the *light*. How important God's Word is; to read it, feed on it, soak it in! Then, to incorporate it into our life, sharing it with others.

God's truth and his light are for all – giving hope and encouragement. For us, yes; but also for the lost, the lonely, the broken, the hungry, the oppressed. We need to share God's truth and light, to help illumine the hearts, minds and souls of people in darkness. It's our post-Christmas gift to them. It's our way of saying we love them, and that God loves them even more. This is our hope for rebuilding the nations, for bringing peace to our brothers and sisters in the world, in our communities. Let's together make music in the hearts of one another; music that sings of this truth and of light. It will be our gift – all because of Christ's glorious incarnation!

Embroidered Garments

You are my King and my God (44:4).

I t's good to remember the past. The psalms often reflect Israelite history – what happened to the children of Israel in days gone by. They speak of how God brought them through difficult times; even how they rejected him, yet God being always faithful – bringing victory for his people. Psalm 44 is this kind of psalm.

We then move to a wedding psalm; a psalm of love. Although it might have been written to celebrate a royal wedding – similar to the royal wedding of Prince William and his beautiful bride, Catherine, in Britain last year – it's more likely a song about the Messiah, Prince of all princes and his bride, the Church. The '*Sons of Korah*' mentioned at the introduction to Psalm 45 may have been the choir that sang this psalm.

This Messiah is *the most excellent of men* (v. 2). He's mighty, clothed with *splendour and majesty* (v. 3); one of *truth, humility and justice* (v. 4). He's to be honoured:

Your throne, O God, will last for ever and ever; a sceptre of justice will be the sceptre of your kingdom (v. 6).

And what about the bride – the Church, us? He loves us more than we could ever imagine. So we should *honour him* and give him all that we are – *for he is your lord* (v. 11).

The Word of God is a 'proposal of marriage' to anyone who will accept the love Christ offers. If we accept, we're clothed with *embroidered garments* (v. 14) and then led to the king *with joy and gladness* (v. 15). What a picture! Presented to the King!

Let's bask in his presence and share this precious truth, this memory – this picture of our embroidered garments – with others:

I will perpetuate your memory through all generations; therefore the nations will praise you for ever and ever (v. 17).

Be Still

God is our refuge and strength, an ever-present help in trouble (v. 1).

I was in Montreal, Quebec, when the horrific terrorist attacks took place in New York on 11 September 2001. We'll never be able to erase the memory of those images that flashed across TV screens worldwide. Several days later, in Montreal, people from all denominations – seeking spiritual refuge and comfort – gathered in a Salvation Army worship centre. As we prayed for the 9/11 victims and the surviving family members, Psalm 46 was read. I believe it was used in many churches around the world that week, and for weeks to follow, as people affirmed:

We will not fear, though the earth give way (v. 2).

The psalmist goes on to speak of a river *whose streams make glad the city of God* (v. 4). Could the river, the stream, be God himself? The peaceful river. The calm stream – in the time of trouble. Any trouble. Any stressful situation. God wants to say to each one of us, as we soon leave this year and move into a new one, that no matter what has happened, or will happen, we're to wait on him:

'Be still, and know that I am God' (v. 10).

Let's take just a few moments to do as God has instructed. Let's meditate upon this particular verse, in intimate communion with him, letting him speak to our heart. Be still.

Prayer

O God, this day, be with and bless those who suffer. Bless our nations. Bless our leaders. Bring healing to our world. Help us not to fear for what lies ahead; but to trust you implicitly with our lives. Help me, this day, to take time – just to be still.

Photo Gallery

Clap your hands, all you nations; shout to God with cries of joy (47:1).

P salm 47 is a corporate song of praise, joy and exaltation. It's very fitting as
we reflect upon the Christmas we just celebrated with family and friends,
and the year that has passed. For God has truly blessed us in so many
wonderful ways. The psalmist insists that we never stop praising God:

Sing praises to God, sing praises; sing praises to our King, sing praises (v. 6).

When we praise God, continuously, it lifts our spirit. When we praise him,
even when things are not always working out perfectly in our lives, it
somehow gets us through – boosting our confidence, affirming our trust in the
Lord; for he knows all, sees all, works through all situations. He *is* to be
greatly exalted (v. 9).

Why is he so worthy of praise? Psalm 48 answers it for us; it's because of
God's unfailing love. No matter what we do, what we say, what we *fail* to do
for him, he loves us. So, the psalmist says:

Within your temple, O God, we meditate on your unfailing love (48:9).

Now think of and reflect upon people you love today. Picture them in your
mind, one by one, and thank God for them. You probably had family
members walk into your 'picture'. Now think of friends. Picture them,
thanking God for them. Ask for God's blessing upon this great 'photo gallery'
of family and friends.

Reflect upon all God has done for you over this past year. Recall the times
you've felt particularly close to him. Add this to the photo gallery. Meditate
upon his goodness, his faithfulness:

*This God is our God for ever and ever; he will be our guide even to the end
(v. 14).*

And let's not rush these precious moments – for they're to be treasured.

The Rising of the Sun

Hear this, all you peoples; listen, all who live in this world (49:1).

D o you ever feel you're speaking, but no one's listening? Perhaps this is how the psalmist was feeling when writing these words. I can picture him standing on a huge rock, a few people gathered around – and him shouting as loud as possible: 'Hear this! Listen!' He hopes some will stop their busy lives long enough to *hear* what he has to say.

Sometimes we may wonder if we're making a difference. We tell others of Christ, of new life in him; but are they turning to faith? Becoming born again, adopted into God's family?

Psalm 50 goes on to say that it's God who summons the earth, calling people unto himself. All we're expected to do is be faithful in sharing the good news of the gospel: by words we say, by the way we live for Christ. Then, we ask the Holy Spirit to convict.

As we continue to pray for souls, we must have faith to believe people will accept Christ as Lord and Saviour:

The Mighty One, God, the LORD, speaks and summons the earth from the rising of the sun to the place where it sets (50:1).

From the rising of the sun . . . In other words, he reaches out, all day long, to the whole earth – calling people to himself. What a glorious picture! And we're to help people *hear* God's call; help them *respond* to his summons. Not just on Sundays; but always.

As we anticipate a brand new year, may we live holy lives, pleasing to him – so people will see Christ in us.

Prayer

Lord, may people's ears be open to hear your glorious message. May I be used, from morning to night, to speak of your great love.

O Worship the King

'As I looked, thrones were set in place, and the Ancient of Days took his seat. His clothing was as white as snow; the hair on his head was white like wool' (v. 9).

The Ancient of Days is a name for God used only in Daniel 7, emphasising his eternality and his sovereignty over time itself:

> O worship the King, all glorious above;
> O gratefully sing his power and his love;
> Our shield and defender, the Ancient of Days,
> Pavilioned in splendour and girded with praise.
> *(SASB 16)*

At the close of 2012, we want to worship our King, we want to praise him for who he is – with all his love, in all his splendour. Through the second and third stanzas of this hymn we're reminded of God's might, grace, wonders, power. The following verse speaks of his care for us, giving us great motivation for the coming year:

> Thy bountiful care what tongue can recite?
> It breathes in the air, it shines in the light,
> It streams from the hills, it descends to the plain,
> And sweetly distils in the dew and the rain.
> (v. 4)

This beautiful imagery, given to us by Robert Grant, emphasises the Lord's tender mercy, *breathing* in the air, *shining* in the light. God's bountiful love for us is evident everywhere!

As we bring this hymn, this year, this book to a close, my prayer is that we'll *all* worship our King. May this be our shared benediction:

> **O measureless Might! Ineffable Love!**
> **While angels delight to hymn thee above,**
> **The humbler creation, though feeble their lays,**
> **With true adoration shall sing to thy praise!**

Notes

1. Charles T. Fritsch, 'The Gospel in the Book of Proverbs', ed. John A. Mackay, *Theology Today*, Vol. 7, 2nd Ed., 1950, pp 169–183, Princeton Theological Seminary, Princeton, New Jersey, USA.
2. Stuart Briscoe, *The Fruit of the Spirit* © 1993 Harold Shaw Publishers, Wheaton, Illinois, USA.
3. *Christianity Today*, 26 March 1976.
4. Joseph C. Aldrich, *Lifestyle Evangelism* © 1981 Multnomah Press, Oregon, USA.

Index

Subscribe . . .

Words of Life is published three times a year:
January–April, May–August and September–December

Four easy ways to subscribe
- By post – simply complete and return the subscription form below
- By phone – +44 (0) 1933 445 445
- Online http://sar.my/wolsubu (for UK) or http://sar.my/wolsubo (for overseas)
- Or visit your local Christian bookshop

SUBSCRIPTION FORM

Name (Miss, Mrs, Ms, Mr)...

Address ....

.... Postcode ....

Tel. No. ....

Email* ....

Annual Subscription Rates
UK £12.50   *Non-UK* £12.50 + £3.50 P&P = £16.00
Please send me .... copy/copies of the next three issues of *Words of Life* commencing with **January–April 2013**

Total: £ .... **I enclose payment by cheque** ☐
Please make cheques payable to *The Salvation Army*

Please debit my Access/Mastercard/Visa/American Express/Switch card

Card No. ☐☐☐☐ ☐☐☐☐ ☐☐☐☐ ☐☐☐☐ ☐☐☐ Expiry date: ___/___

Security No. ☐☐☐ **Issue number (Switch only)** _____

Cardholder's signature: .... Date: ....

Please send this form and any cheques to: The Mail Order Department, Salvationist Publishing and Supplies, 66–78 Denington Road, Denington Industrial Estate, Wellingborough, Northamptonshire NN8 2QH, UK

☐ *We would like to keep in touch with you by placing you on our mailing list. If you would prefer not to receive correspondence from us, please tick this box. The Salvation Army does not sell or lease its mailing lists.